MAN, WOMAN, AND MARRIAGE

Consulting Editors

The Editor

A L A N L . G R E Y is an Associate Professor in the Clinical Psychology Program of the Graduate School of Arts and Sciences at Fordham University. He received his B.A. in sociology from the City College of the City University of New York, his M.A. in sociology from Columbia University, and his Ph.D. in psychology from the University of Chicago. Dr. Grey is also on the staff of the William Alanson White Institute of Psychoanalysis as a Research Coordinator and Supervisor of Psychotherapy in the Blue Collar Treatment Program of the Low Cost Clinic. In addition to his teaching and research, Dr. Grey is a practicing psychoanalyst and psychotherapist. He has published several articles in professional journals, contributed to several books, and edited *Class and Personality in Society* for Atherton Press.

Man, Woman,

EDITED BY

AND MARRIAGE

SMALL GROUP PROCESS IN THE FAMILY

Alan L. Grey

ATHERTON PRESS

New York 1970

Man, Woman, and Marriage:
Small Group Process in the Family
edited by Alan L. Grey

Address all inquiries to:
Atherton Press, Inc.
70 Fifth Avenue
New York 10011

Library of Congress Catalog Card Number: 72–105607

FIRST EDITION

Manufactured in the United States of America
DESIGNED BY LORETTA LI

Contents

MAN, WOMAN, AND MARRIAGE

Introduction

ALAN L. GREY

KEY ISSUES

Why marry? Some ponder that question because of avant-garde views about the relations between the sexes or, from a very different moral standpoint, because they are drawn to a cloistered religious life. But most continue to accept the institution of marriage for themselves despite the considerable flux in other contemporary social institutions. And, for such people, the image of a happy family endures as more than merely an incidental goal. Sociologists report that increasingly the home is regarded as a major source of the happiness and emotional security we seek (see, for example, Potter, 1954). This would seem to provide a strong impetus for the study of marital life—to tease out the secrets of matrimonial success.

Actually, marriage has not been given attention in the relevant social sciences proportional to the apparent general interest in the topic. True, the first paper in the present collection is addressed to a problem rather like "Whom shall I marry?" (Winch, Ktsanes, and Ktsanes, 1954), and so are a number of other essays cited in our bibliography. On the other hand, studies of details of daily interaction after marriage are relatively recent and still quite meager. For all too long, the focus of much family research has been sadly parallel to that of the standard movie scenario. It provides close-ups of the boy, of the girl, and of their courtship but fades out without a portrayal of their life together after the nuptials.

Our collection gives evidence, however, that certain promising developments in the past few years have been directed at correcting the deficiency. These are not practical investigations, and they do not tackle problems of the order of "How can I be a good partner to my spouse?" Usually, attention is on more theoretical issues and even here, it hardly can be claimed that there has been a smooth and consistent accumulation of knowledge. Far more often than they arrive at answers, the experts have had to content themselves with reformulations of their questions. Still there is a continuity and even some encouraging progress in the debate itself. So we focus here on the central controversies in the study of husband-wife interaction and decline pretensions to final wisdom.

This objective is not completely modest. By following the living edge of research effort, the intention is to achieve a deeper comprehension of basic issues than is available from textbook summaries alone. To help the unfamiliar reader on his journey, this introductory essay reviews key facts and ideas relevant to the selected papers that follow. The studies themselves are linked to each other not only in subject matter but in their progressive exploration of what might be called the psychosocial aspects of marriage.

The term "psychosocial" was coined to indicate an orientation that cuts across conventional disciplinary boundaries, raising issues provocative to a heterogeneous range of specialists. Clinical psychologists, sociologists, anthropologists, and social psychologists are among those whose interests often converge in the exploration of marriage. To come somewhat closer to defining the area, psychosocial research studies aspects of human behavior not readily explained in terms of social usages alone, nor yet as purely intrapsychic needs and processes. Family relationships, for instance, are affected in part by the social circumstances to which the members must adapt, in part by the specific roles expected of husbands, wives, and children, and in part by their individual needs and characters. With so many variables inevitably influencing the situation, it has seemed wise to limit our inquiry somewhat, confining the selection of papers to the American scene.

The central theme linking the essays is one that runs through much of social science. It is the quest for better descriptions of the actual and immediate processes by which the several participants in a social field—in this case, the family—affect one another. It must be granted that this statement of the task still is not sufficiently sharp to define a focus for a research project. The fact is that while all of the reprinted papers pursue the same issue, they do not seek their answers via the same single question. As knowledge has accumulated it has suggested new frames of inquiry. Just how one question has grown out of another will become more evident via perusal of the succession of studies to follow. The questions themselves might be summarized in these terms:

1. In seeking a mate, is one attracted to a person with similar personality characteristics or to one with complementary characteristics?
2. Can different types of families be identified, each with its own pattern of husband-wife interaction?
3. How is the response style of a given family member affected by the presence or absence of other members?

A fourth concern relevant to all of these ways of framing the central issue is:

4. What methods are best suited to the investigation of the foregoing questions?

Having outlined the field of inquiry here, the next three introductory sections will survey work done prior to 1954, the publication year of our first selection (Winch, Ktsanes, and

Ktsanes, 1954). First there is a review of earlier theories of social interaction, followed by hypotheses specific to mate selection, and then by typical research approaches in these matters. Afterward, the introduction continues with a separate commentary on each study reprinted in this volume. The discussion of each individual paper can be identified by its heading, which provides a capsule statement of the theme in the paper most relevant to the main thread of our exposition.

GENERAL THEORIES OF SOCIAL INTERACTION

To consider, even briefly, all the important theories of interpersonal relations available in 1954 would be a formidable task. Among the more viable ones at the time were various stimulus response formulations dominant in academic psychology (Lambert, 1954), the "field theory" of Kurt Lewin and his followers (Deutsch, 1954), Freud's psychoanalysis (1949), the neo-Freudian "interpersonal relations" theory of Sullivan (1947) and "role theory" views (Sarbin, 1954) designed to bridge the gap between psychological and sociological approaches to social behavior. The problem is reduced sharply if our exposition is limited to those actually employed in systematic family research. That is because most American marriage studies at the time were confined to the single discipline of sociology (Nye and Bayer, 1963; Burchinal, 1964, p. 623). Moreover, the majority of these sociologists can be grouped within a few theoretical persuasions.

An influential paper by Hill and Hansen (1960) identifies five "schools" of *sociologists* in the marriage field. Two of them, the "Institutional" and "Developmental" approaches, with their respective emphases on cross-cultural and longitudinal studies, are not essentially conflicting theories but complementary ways of gathering data about family life. Since their perspectives are largely outside the immediate concerns of this volume, only brief reference will be made to their work. A third "Structural–Functional" viewpoint will be considered in connection with papers after 1954, in our collection, as will theories from sources outside sociology (such as social psychology and psychoanalysis). Of the two remaining schools, the "Symbolic Interactionists" (sometimes called "role theorists") were particularly influential before Winch and relevant to understanding his ideas. They will be reviewed here together with the fifth or "Situational Approach" which is sufficiently similar (see Stryker, 1964) so that it need not be treated separately.

Symbolic interactionism numbers among its principle figures W. I. Thomas (1927), George Herbert Mead (1934), and John Dewey (1930), all of the University of Chicago. Even William James (1892), and more currently, Erving Goffman (1961), can be added to the list. From this roster it will be evident that views within the school have been almost as varied as they are distinguished. But they share a common emphasis on the inner psychological system of the *self,* one's enduring sense of personal identity, as essential to an understanding of human social behavior. Although the *self* refers to what most would regard as internal and subjective experiences, early interactionists were wary of describing it in terms of thought processes. Contemporary behaviorists had attacked the notion of *thinking* as too inaccessible for respectable scientific study and the interactionists were impressed by some of their arguments.

To avoid the pitfalls of subjectivity, Mead stated his observations in the language of interpersonal interactions rather than intrapsychic processes and referred to mental phenomena as "symbolic" or "verbal" operations. Although he studied intrapsychic events dismissed by the behaviorists of his day, Mead still saw himself as "behavioristic in the sense of starting off with an observable activity—the dynamic, on-going social process, and the social acts which are its component elements" (Mead, 1934, p. 7). His stress on the importance of interactions between people—for example, parent and child—in shaping the personality was, of course, more than a terminological gambit. It was a deeply held and sensitively explored conviction. Hence the label "symbolic interactionism" is apt for him and those who share his views. This emphasis on the close examination of immediate face-to-face social transactions as the most suitable means for understanding personality is a second hallmark of symbolic interactionism, and one which has increasingly been employed in recent research. For a sprightly criticism of the position, one can consult Zicklin (1968), who finds its premises still pertinent if incomplete.

Several research approaches have been used by interactionists to implement their premises. From the first, Cooley (1909), Mead, and others gave much attention to informal observation of everyday experiences of the child, presented in anecdotal form and then analyzed. Their concern was with unraveling the mystery of how man becomes socialized. The term refers, of course, to "the interactional process by which the individual is taught his place in the social order" (Hinsie and Shatzky, 1940, p. 490). Out of his experience in learning roles the child was seen as developing a "concept of self" which might be more or less satisfying and harmonious with role expectations, depending on the nature of role-training experiences. As in psychoanalysis, family relationships were treated as crucial because of their formative impact during the early impressionable years. Goffman has continued in much the same style of naturalistic observation, although he points to the continuing influence of social role definitions on the self-regard of the adult.

Perhaps the first sociologist to do a major study of husband-wife relationships in a systematic fashion, using statistical controls, was the interactionist E. W. Burgess, also of the University of Chicago. Apart from his many other contributions to sociology, Burgess's two books on marriage, *Promoting Success or Failure in Marriage* (1939, with L. Cottrell), and *Engagement and Marriage* (1953, with P. Wallin), were pioneering works. These landmarks in the field generated many similar researches. Handel's review article (1965), reprinted in this volume, trenchantly describes the premises and limitations of the Burgess contribution. Most of Burgess's data were obtained from carefully designed questionnaires given separately to each member of the couples studied.

A third mode of interactional study, and one much favored by this school, is the systematic examination of social processes in small face-to-face groups. A recent poll of "forty interactionists whose contributions to the literature have established them as leading spokesmen for this position" brings out that while they may differ on other issues, all agree about the pertinence of small group observation (Vaughan and Reynolds, 1968, p. 208). Their position "stresses face-to-face small group activities," or again "its concepts were developed in the context of short episodes of interaction, or with respect to socialization" (Vaughan and Reynolds, 1968, p. 209). It is an interesting and curious fact, however, that small group methods were not applied to family research until relatively recently, even by the very interactionists so interested in both.

The term "small group methods" refers here to systematically designed and quantified research procedures (see, e.g., Shepherd, 1964). Mead, Thomas, and others had, of course, considered how individual family members influence each other but they had relied on informal observations and reports. In anthropology, too, brilliant clinical-style records of parent–child interactions like those of Bateson and Mead (1942) led to a new awareness of the great influence of nonverbal as well as deliberate verbal communication in face-to-face contacts. *The Silent Language*, by Hall (1959) offers not only a useful bibliography containing studies in this area before 1954 but also an excellent exposition of the social influence of behavioral cues. As one source for their sensitive observations, these anthropologists cited the "interpersonal theory" of psychoanalyst Harry Stack Sullivan. The similarity of Sullivan's ideas to those of interactionist W. I. Thomas and field theory psychologist Kurt Lewin was sufficiently noteworthy to provide themes for Otto Klineberg (1952), Murphy and Cattell (1952) and Cottrell and Foote (1952). These anthropologists and psychoanalysts, as well as many of their colleagues, added to the fund of ideas available in the social sciences to investigators like Winch et al. If they are treated only briefly here, it is because their researches were not of the formally designed sort which are our immediate interest.

THEORIES OF MATE SELECTION AND MARITAL INTERACTION

Symbolic interactionists, before Winch et al., had recognized that enduring face-to-face relationships, as in the family, require complex processes of mutual response and accommodation. They realized that such ties become patterned into more or less stable small social systems, with varying degrees of flexibility. Also they stressed that accurate description of these processes demands observation of interaction from moment to moment, with equal attention to nonverbal aspects of behavior. Nor did this focus on the immediate act ignore that individuals bring certain response predispositions to any social situation. Close attention to the *self* was, in effect, a concern with an aspect of *personality*. While the specific term "personality" has not always been used by researchers into interpersonal processes, a significant number of them have shared the assumption that "each person has certain pervasive psychological needs which can best be gratified through interaction with another possessing certain personality characteristics (Marlowe and Gergen, 1969, p. 623).

Although such propositions provide a valuable orientation for research, they obviously are not specific enough to answer such questions as: What (personality) type of spouse probably will be chosen by a given (personality) category of men or women? What sort of mate is most likely to achieve a mutually satisfying relationship with a given kind of person? Controversy in the field has centered far more around issues of this sort than on the more basic but widely accepted generalizations summarized in the previous paragraph. By the 1950s, sociologists had developed their theories sufficiently and accumulated enough research data so that they were prepared to offer some answers about marital choice. The main findings, including those of Burgess and Cottrell (1949) and of Burgess and Wallin (1953) were to the effect that mate selection is homogamous.

The term "homogamy" refers "to the observation that, in general, husbands and wives in American families resemble one another in various physical, psychological social characteristics" (Burchinal, 1964, p. 645). "Endogamy" and "assortive mating" are other terms sometimes used to indicate the same process of choosing a partner similar to oneself (see Murdock, 1949, for further specialized terminology relevant to marriage). The data supporting the hypothesis of homogamous selection (see Burchinal, 1964, especially pp. 645–658) range in content from premarital residential propinquity to similarity in race, age, religion, social status, physical and psychological characteristics. For many sociologists and psychologists, these findings were eminently plausible and did not require further explanation. This was particularly true of the many who were content to see human behavior as sheeplike, conditioned conformity to the group. (This sociological orientation is analyzed acutely by Inkeles, 1959).

It was Robert Winch who first seriously challenged the homogamy principle in the sociological journals. His theory of complementarity (1954)—the first paper in our collection—granted that some degree of similarity is the usual prerequisite for mutual attraction, limiting mate selection to a "field of eligibles," to use his phrase. But he proceeded to argue that from within this field one seeks a spouse whose traits are opposite to one's own in a fashion capable of supplementing felt needs and deficiencies. A fuller statement of Winch's position can be found in the article itself (Winch, Ktsanes, and Ktsanes, 1954). It is more useful here to focus instead on a survey of background information contributory to his thinking. Among the attractions of the Winch formulation were its possibilities for integrating a rich mine of observations both sociological and psychological. Its relative complexity even seemed more consonant with the recognized intricacy of the psychosocial phenomena it attempted to explain than were simple assertions about assortive mating.

Consider, first, the sociological evidence. Winch had stressed that especially characteristic of American marriage is its emphasis on personal choice as the criterion for selection, on love as the *sine qua non*. Why this special emphasis on romantic attraction in the United States? As long ago as the nineteenth century, economists like Marx and sociologists like Ferdinand Tönnies (trans. 1957) were struck by a syndrome of changes in social institutions which seemed to occur wherever the economy shifted from the traditional agrarian mold to modern urban industrial production. Because of its outstanding technological advancement, American society commonly has been regarded as a pronounced example of such changes and, as part of that society, so has the American family.

Among the consequences, "the family's economic, educational, religious, recreational and protective tasks have been reduced considerably," according to the sociological consensus (Bardis, 1964, p. 458). Attitudes of family members undergo a progressive narrowing of kinship loyalties, moving from extended family allegiances to a nuclear family orientation. The term "nuclear family" designates a household consisting of husband, wife, and their own children while the "extended family" is any group of relatives more extensive than the nuclear set, who live together under the same authority. More detailed descriptions of cross-cultural and developmental variations in the family as an institution may be found in Christensen's authoritative *Handbook of Marriage and the Family* (1964), particularly in the chapters by Christensen, Mogey, and Zelditch. Limiting ourselves here to a brief overview of the American family, we can turn also to David Potter's *People of Plenty* (1954, p. 204), which presents a widely respected view:

> when abundance began to diminish the economic duties imposed upon the housewife . . . the romantic or emotional factor assumed increasing importance . . . emotional harmony became

the principal criterion of success in a marriage, while lack of such harmony became a major threat to the existence of the marriage . . . the children of enduring marriages, as well as the children of divorce, must inevitably feel the impact of this increased emphasis upon emotional factors, must inevitably sense the difference in the foundations of the institution which holds their universe in place.

More recent research has challenged the closeness of the relationship between romantic love and large industry (see, e.g., Goode, 1963; Lantz et al., 1968), but even these newer findings do not seriously question the importance of romantic love in the United States.

Moving to the work of psychologists, Winch's theory also fits well with much that had been observed clinically by psychoanalysts and other specialists with a psychodynamic orientation (e.g., Oberndorf, 1938; Ackerman, 1954). His debt to this group and to Henry Murray in particular is explicitly acknowledged. It is reflected, too, in his use of projective techniques to tap dimensions of the mind overlooked by many of his precursors. The psychodynamic literature indeed suggested that at the psychopathological extreme one often found that neurotic spouses chose and remained with each other to satisfy complementary immature needs. At the healthy pole, too, Foote's paper on love (1953) spoke of the optimal marriage as one in which "the success of the marriage is judged by the degree to which each partner contributes reciprocally to the continuous development of the other" (p. 251).

Winch's thesis attracted considerable interest, as can be seen from Tharp's subsequent review (1963) elsewhere in this volume. Without reiterating the readily available contents of that review, it is pertinent to note here that the complementarity hypothesis was respected not only for proposing an alternative to the prevailing explanations but also for its psychologically richer and more persuasive formulation of the husband–wife relationship. Whether or not the theory was accepted, it moved family study into the more genuinely cross-disciplinary orientation it requires.

Not long after Winch's 1955 paper, for instance, a well-known social psychologist, Theodore Newcomb, was moved to discuss the complementarity principle, although heretofore marriage research had attracted little attention in social psychology. Newcomb's 1956 paper was among the first to consider the relevance of data about mate selection to other processes of social attraction, such as friendships. With the expansion of interest in these phenomena, the term "interpersonal attractiveness" has been used as a comprehensive rubric for the wider field, including sociometric research (see Lindzey and Byrne, 1969). When Newcomb described Winch's reciprocal principle, his first characterization of it was as "surely . . . a plausible notion" (1956, p. 577), but then he proceeded to refute it. That refutation is worthy of re-examination here because it was an especially sophisticated and influential defense of the homogamy position.

The heart of Newcomb's argument rested on his view of the communication process. This focus may have been only coincidentally reminiscent of symbolic interactionism but it treated social interplay in terms more amenable to systematic test than had the interactionists. As Newcomb put it, (1) "the life history of every human being has made accurate communication rewarding far more often than punishing" and (2) "increased similarity in some degree and manner is the regular accompaniment of accurate communication" (1956, p. 575). He then proceeded to argue that Winch's position actually was only a special case within his own theory. That is, complementarity was interpreted as one form of similarity in which both partners have "similar attitudes to the effect that one of them should be assertive and the other receptive" (p. 579). This was not the only time that the controversy was to be marked by what may strike one as feats of verbal juggling. For instance, the interchange between Tharp and Levinger, reprinted in this collection, captures some of that quality.

And yet, in a different sense than he intended, Newcomb's theory shared a most important characteristic with that of Winch and, indeed, with most of those on both sides of the similarity–complementarity debate of the 1950s. Both views, as then formulated, implicitly picture the normal personality as having an essentially fixed and unchanging profile of characteristics, such as might be measured by a psychometric test. This pattern is treated as if it endures through time and space, independently of social circumstances and other influences. In Winch's complementarity model, any given personality has contours as set as those of jigsaw-puzzle pieces. The goal of mate selection is to juxtapose oneself with a reciprocally shaped personality for best results. For Newcomb, the same image holds, except that the task is not to dovetail the pieces but rather to match them so that character profiles coincide maximally. Note, too, that neither theory makes a clear distinction between processes of attraction and the subsequent processes by which people learn to live with each other as a married couple. Is it wise to assume that the same qualities which are most effective in courtship are equally relevant to the best mutual adaptation afterward?

The rigidity implied in this conception of personality is more appropriate to current notions about psychopathological states than to optimal relationships. In fact, our paper by Cohen and others (1968) examines seriously disturbed families to test the existence of precisely such rigidity. Neither the similarity nor the complementarity model, at least in these earlier forms, provides for personal growth or for "love as the interpersonal conditions optimal for self-transcendence" (Foote, 1953, p. 250). Because of such shortcomings, and others to be described later, similarity studies are not among the most promising current avenues of family research and are not represented in the later part of this collection.

Obviously, not everyone would agree with this view, for work along those lines has continued. Some of the more important examples after 1955 are cited here briefly for those who wish to pursue the matter further. After his 1956 paper, Newcomb continued to study social attraction (1959, 1961) with continuing confirmation of his position. Its emphasis on conscious attitudes links it with other studies focused on cognitive processes, such as Festinger's well-known cognitive dissonance theory (1957) and Heider's balance theory as applied to mutual attraction (1958). All of these researches have tested a similarity principle with confirmatory results. Recent reviews by Marlowe and Gergen (1969) and by Lindzey and Byrne (1969) provide additional examples.

An important limitation of this type of inquiry lies not in the falsity of the hypothesis, for it seems to contain a substantial truth. The difficulty is rather in a selective inattention to significant aspects of interpersonal relations, a psychological incompleteness. By confining themselves to intellective phenomena, such inquiries neglect to explore other potential influences which may be even more powerful in affecting social behavior. There is much evidence to suggest that the need for the partner's agreement is only a part or sometimes an epiphenomenon of more fundamental human needs. The very research methods typical of these investigations seriously limit their capacity to explore, as the next section makes more evident.

PROBLEMS OF RESEARCH METHOD

The first of the four questions raised earlier, concerned with factors in mate selection, has taken the major part of our attention thus far. Others, dealing with more specific aspects of the relationship between spouses, had barely been investigated in a systematic fashion before 1960. In fact, these matters had not yet been stated in readily testable terms. Here we come to the fourth issue on our list, but hardly the least important. It is the problem of research methods to implement already existing conceptions of family interaction. Specific theories may die but the development of appropriate methodology arises anew with each fresh conceptualization.

How does one trace and measure a sequence of mutual responses? The reader may be suprised by Winch's procedures. They do not include any observation of husband and wife together, nor do they go beyond verbal statements to total styles of response. There is a temptation to assume that he ignored the prior work of Burgess and other leading exponents of interactionism. This conclusion might be reinforced especially after one reads Burgess's (1926) paper, or the quotations from it in Handel's (1964) review article included here.

To single out Winch for special criticism on this score, however, would do him an injustice. Because his research tactics were quite typical of the marriage field, they merit review in this section rather than solely in connection with his particular paper. Handel puts Winch's relation to Burgess trenchantly when he states that "Burgess's (1926) concept [of the family as an interacting system] has received great veneration and reiteration in family sociology but for about a quarter of a century little effort seems to have been made to pursue its implications." What Handel does not mention is that even Burgess and his school had been guilty of the same deficiency. Stryker (1964), an objective spokesman for interactionism, has himself observed that:

> Unfortunately, the techniques which have been best developed and are most frequently used are individual in their orientation and derivation: attitude scales, questionnaires, case histories. As a consequence, in general, characterizations of relational phenomena have been inadequate. By way of illustration, marital success—clearly a product of a relationship—has been indexed by responses of married pairs taken individually even by researchers who are most sensitive to the requirements of symbolic interaction theory. Burgess and Cottrell's (1939) pioneer work in this area is a case in point (p. 154).

In short, interactionists did not study interaction. To illustrate the crucial necessity for noting what people *do* as well as what they *say*, no neater example is needed than one finds in the hiatus between theory and practice among these researchers. Nor is the inconsistency confined to one group. We all realize that, for various reasons, men may portray themselves inaccurately. What is curious is that so many social scientists have been unconcerned with this phenomenon and with the consequent limitations of self-report. Such unconcern is reflected, at least, in the wide reliance on self-report for marriage research. In a questionnaire, a husband may tell us about his wife's angry temper as a source of marital difficulty. At the same time, he gives no clue that he elicits her anger by his fault-finding or unresponsiveness. Even his partner may not be able to supply the missing information, particularly if the provocation is his coldness rather than explicit actions. She may be unaware of his defenses and ashamed of her lack of charm. Beyond that, neither one may recognize that the gulf between them is one of the attractions of the marriage because of discomforts with intimacy. To uncover this process, more sensitive devices may be required, such as projective techniques or minute observation.

These possibilities raise an important question about how much theory and method unwittingly played into each other in earlier studies. Was confirmation of the homogamy theory produced by artifact in that prevailing methods failed to detect important areas of fact? Could it be that questionnaires administered to each spouse separately are relatively effective in registering gross social similarities between them but inadequate to trace reciprocal psychological interplay? How much the vision of the experts was blurred in this fashion is not readily measured. Simpler to estimate is the actual prevalence of questionnaire approaches in past marital studies. Nye and Bayer (1963) found them to be the principle tools more than half the time, as against about one half of one percent relying on direct observation. Obviously, questionnaires have their attractions. They require less time, money, and ingenuity than observation or projective devices. They also fit in quite readily with conceptions of personality framed *in vacuo*, as it were, postulating a fixed pattern without allowing for possible major variations elicited in response to varying social contexts.

At its worst, the questionnaire has been used to spare the researcher from the burden of describing behavior by passing on the responsibility of self-description to the respondents. In frankly recognizing the limited utility of such data, the investigator finds himself confronted by the formidable difficulties of his chosen field. How to induce husband and wife to expose their most private reactions? Even after they are willing, how to provide an atmosphere in which they can lose self-consciousness and behave in typical ways? Then, since it is impossible to record literally everything, and unwieldy to analyze it all, how to select the psychosocially most significant aspects of a complex interaction sequence?

Perhaps it is their very awareness of such complexities that deterred psychologists from active participation in family research until quite recently. That sociologists have far outnumbered them in this area is readily revealed by considering the names of the four journals selected by Nye and Bayer for their survey of marriage research cited above. The publications are *American Journal of Sociology, Social Forces,* the *American Sociological Review,* and *Marriage and Family Living.* The obvious sociological flavor of this list cannot be attributed merely to the professional bias of the authors. Until a short time ago, it was quite accurate to say that "the research literature consists almost exclusively of sociological studies and, although its roots reach back into the early part of this century, the bulk of research is less than two decades old" (Burchinal, 1964, p. 623).

That methodological complexities were a major deterrent for psychologists is my own surmise. And yet, how else to explain their long neglect of phenomena so psychologically pertinent? Where the folk customs of sociologists have tempted them to major themes, albeit vaguely stated at times, the tradition of the psychologist has been focused on precision of method. Ever since their struggle to emerge from the brow of philosophy, academic psychologists have wanted to distinguish their own activities as amenable to scientific measurement on a par with the "natural" sciences. This has given an edge to exactness of measurement over meaningfulness. There has been a tendency to study artificial groups under circumstances of laboratory control, rather than complex social groups like the family, involving intense and tangled interactions over long periods. As a team of social psychologists assessed the state of affairs during the 1950s (Lorge et al., 1958, p. 570), "The researches to date tend to treat the *ad hoc* group solving a trivial task as a prototype of the fully traditional group solving a very important problem."

It is a dubious strategy to give procedural concerns an inflexible priority over meaningfulness of the subject matter. That they can be overcome is attested by the remarkable work of Masters and Johnson in penetrating that once most secret aspect of man's mating behavior, in the *Human Sexual Response* (1966). It might even be claimed that the neglect of marital transactions because of difficulties in their exploration is more unfortunate than the opposite bias, which tackles profound themes via shallow data, as in the case of some questionnaire studies. Both extremes, however, make it evident that effective research requires a judicious mating of method with theory for the meaningful translation of ideas into research operations. At different stages in the development of a field the need for theoretical reformulations and for methodological improvements will alternate in their relative importance for the advancement of knowledge. This is borne out in our own series of studies.

Within a decade after the stimulus provided by Winch's new theory, it had become clear that the liveliest developments in family study revolved around certain innovations of research technique. Beginning with Handel's (1965) paper in our collection, the reader can witness a branching out into new directions. At that point our attention departs from investigations that continue along the question-and-answer path and pursue the old similarity-complementarity theme. Such work does go on into the present so obviously it is a continuing controversy for some experts. Nevertheless, the focus of our own choice of papers shifts with Handel to other researchers who are concentrating on newer techniques to illuminate a more fluidly formulated view of family interaction. The whole story is best told, however, by discussion of the specific papers that compose our selection.

Assessing the System from Its Separate Parts

In a footnote at the beginning of his 1954 paper, Winch notes that his "theory of complementary needs may be extended beyond mate selection and the dyad . . . in explaining the formation of cliques within groups, in selecting working teams as for bomber crews and the like." Clearly the intention is to study mate selection as only a "special case" in the larger field of group dynamics. Indeed it is precisely under the title of Group Dynamics that his work later was evaluated in the *Annual Review of Psychology* (Gerard and Miller, 1967), together with other researches it had generated. His plan was to make specific predictions about how one partner "will behave with" the other on the basis of the complementarity principle, as a test of its adequacy.

How to investigate these dyadic interactions? As is already evident, even the symbolic interactionists who were especially interested in such phenomena had not found satisfactory procedures for the exploration of husband–wife relationships. One of them confessed as recently as 1968 "The great difficulty with symbolic interaction lies in operationalizing concepts and other methodological problems" (Vaughan and Reynolds, 1968, p. 209). Not that Winch relied on their example. He did not count himself in that school or fit any other typical sociological orientation, although more recently he has joined with the structural functional school (1963, p. v). In 1954 his face was turned toward psychoanalysis and to clinical procedures associated with it, for his investigation.

What special help could Freud offer him in the task of studying dyadic interaction? For one thing, the Viennese physician had dramatically called attention to a great hidden area of psychic activity, beyond what a research subject can tell to his observer or even admit to himself. It is to these unconscious processes that we must look, as well as to direct communications, if we are to predict accurately, said Freud. This principle was integral to Winch's position. Although some of his ideas were to change in the decade following this study, Winch still underscored that he "continues to make use of what the writer [Winch] views as Freud's major contribution—his emphasis on unconscious motivation" (Winch, 1963, p. v). By adding the dimensions of the "deeper levels of personality" to his research, he hoped to uncover previously overlooked patterns of complementarity.

Thought processes are notoriously difficult to study for they cannot be observed directly, save by the thinker himself. Hence some psychologists have dismissed the entire subject as unscientific. And unconscious mental activity presents even more formidable obstacles because, by definition, it is invisible even to its creator. Clinicians faced with this seeming impasse had found their solutions in the use of clinical interviews and in projective techniques (e. g., TAT), among other devices. Very sensibly, Winch borrowed their devices and adapted them for systematic research. In a sequel to the 1954 paper, which reported more complete findings (Winch, 1955), it became evident that the projective road to the unconscious had failed him.

Neither in these papers nor in his later textbook did Winch attempt to explain the failure of these clinical methods. In fact, some years later he minimized the contradictory results of other investigators (reported in Tharp, 1963) as due to their failure to use his methods (Winch, 1963, p. 592–593n)!

The concept of unconsciousness is so closely wedded to projective research in the minds of some that zero results may seem to them to imply the nonexistence or irrelevance of unconscious processes. Others recognize that "unconscious" ideation is not identical with testing procedures developed to detect them. They accept the considerable evidence that such devices have not, on the whole, proven very useful thus far (see, for example, Kleinmuntz, 1967, chapters. 9, 10). They point to other avenues for the detection of dissociated processes, avenues which have yielded more promising results. Neo-Freudian psychoanalysts, for instance, stress the utility of clues derived from direct and careful observation of interpersonal behavior, considered in *conjunction* with intrapsychic ideation (Sullivan, 1947).

Such an alternative approach had not yet occurred to Winch by 1963, nor to several of his critics whom we are about to consider. This, despite the fact that during the 1950s there was a rapid development within the social sciences of devices for the direct measurement of group interaction (see Lindzey, 1954, especially chapters. 10, 22, 24; also Shepherd, 1964). Indeed one man already had studied the family as a small group in 1954, as Handel (1965) indicates, but his inspiration was in advance of the field (Strodtbeck, 1951, 1954).

FROM SIMILARITY-COMPLEMENTARITY TO STRUCTURAL-FUNCTIONALISM

From his vantage point of almost a decade (1954 to 1963), Tharp is able to provide an informative perspective on Winch's work. Citing contrary findings of later investigations, and specifying flaws in Winch's research design, he finds the complementarity studies less satisfying as an investigation than as a theoretical orientation. As for the theory, without accepting it, he appreciates its conceptual step toward Parsons and Bales (1955). Their approach is called "role theory" and, indeed, the idea of "role" is an integral part of it. But the role concept is so widely and variously used by sociologists that it can prove more confusing than identifying. For instance, role theory sometimes connotes symbolic interactionism whereas, in the case of Parsons and Bales, their own distinct school is called the "structural-functional" orientation. In short, the particular role theory supported by Tharp is that of the structural-functionalists, and in Winch he saw a kindred spirit.

Tharp's assessment was confirmed by Winch himself, during the same year (1963) in the second edition of the Winch text, *The Modern Family*. Its preface asserted that "The point of view is structural-functional" (p. v). What virtues inhere in functionalism, especially the Parsons variety, to have won it an amazing number of adherents—in this case, even pulling one from an orientation of his own invention? Tharp explains in his preface, concentrating on more concrete implications of functionalism for family study. For one thing, Parsons and Bales depict the American family as one in which there is "power-equalization" between husband and wife. They are able to relate the shift to broader changes in authority structure throughout American society during the past century.

Moving from power distribution to another dimension of family organization, these functionalists divide functions within the home into "instrumental" and "expressive" kinds. A sort of role complementarity is implied by their discussion. In his instrumental capacity, the American husband undertakes primary responsibility for practical tasks essential to family survival, notably the economic burden and related arrangements. The wife usually is more concerned with facilitation of intrafamilial contacts and, in that connection, with the expression of love. This portrayal of dimensions enriches the formal discussion of family life, providing a schema which brings it closer to everyday experience than abstractions like "homogamy" and "heterogamy." According to Zelditch, the Parsons–Bales picture of sex-role specialization also fits experience in many cultures, being applicable to a high proportion of the 56 he surveyed (1955).

Beyond that, functionalism appeals to sociologists because it provides a formulation linking the most diverse aspects of social behavior. Growing out of Parsons' "general theory of action" (1951), this orientation treats interpersonal patterns as equilibria between internal human organic and external social circumstances, including the family "system" and the larger social context of which it is a part. Its integrative scope is indicated by its inclusion of principles drawn from psychoanalysis, on the one hand (Parsons, 1958) and from economics on the other (Parsons and Shils, 1951, especially pp. 28ff.). Thus it did not require that Winch abandon his interest in unconscious processes and complementary response patterns, but put these phenomena into an encompassing frame of reference.

The division of American husband-wife roles described by Parsons and Bales is strikingly similar to Bales' earlier (1953) characterization of roles in small discussion groups. His method of "interaction process analysis," which calls for observers to classify each act of the group participants into one of twelve categories, has been widely applied. It was typical of a larger trend noted in a major review article (Kelly and Thibaut, 1954). As Kelley and Thibaut put it, investigators "of the last decade have placed much greater emphasis upon observations of the ongoing stream of behavior (interactions and communications) which constitute the problem-solving process" (p. 779). It may seem puzzling that while Bales both studied families and extended his role typology from small discussion groups to the home, neither he nor anyone else (except Strodtbeck) made a parallel transfer of interaction research methods.

This puzzle is nowhere more pertinent than in a perusal of Tharp's review article. The absence in it of references to direct interaction studies is a reasonable reflection of the actual situation. As his survey indicates, the device most often used to overcome this deficiency was to explore the mathematical relationship between test scores instead of the psychological relation between the spouses! Some of the efforts to make test score relationships substitute for human interactions resulted in truly heroic exercises. Note the "Index of Strain" which is "the cube root of the sum of the differences between the ranks the subjects assign to each role" or Q sorts of "wife's prediction x husband's self-perception; and the husband's prediction x wife's perception of him."

DOES CONCEPT CLARIFICATION LEAD BACK TO COMPLEMENTARITY?

Levinger's vigorous critique makes apparent some of the muddiness in key concepts of mate selection. Is it not possible that husband and wife might be both similar and complementary to each other, he asks. This excellent point then is developed in a somewhat labored fashion, rooted more in logic than in psychology. Even so, he neglects to make an obvious logical point—that the most direct answer to his own question might lie in examination of spouses together. Or, turning to psychological data, Levinger could have found considerable support and descriptive clarification of his position in the literature of dynamic psychiatry. It provides a classic example of how two similar people might respond to each other complementarily, in descriptions of the so-called sado-masochistic character or the more common "normal" pattern of authoritarian character. An authoritarian person "admires authority and tends to submit to it but at the same time he wants to be an authority himself and have others submit to him" (Fromm, 1941, p. 164).

As the attention of therapists has shifted more and more to group treatment, illustrative examples of simultaneous similarity and complementarity have increased in the psychodynamic literature. Among the most widely known adaptations of psychoanalysis to group treatment has been the "transactional analysis" approach of Eric Berne (1961, 1964). For certain kinds of stereotyped maneuvers between people, he coined the term "games." In his definition, a game is any "recurring set of transactions, often repetitious, superficially plausible, with a concealed motivation" (1964, p. 48), hidden because its objective is childlike or pathological gratification which the "player" finds too shameful to acknowledge to others or to himself. Berne notes that "Almost any game can form the scaffolding for married life and family living" (1964, p. 92) and describes several alleged to be especially relevant under such picturesque titles as "If It Weren't for You," and "Harried." Like Levinger, he considers that mates may be both complementary and similar at the same time, for "people who play a certain game can potentially play any of the roles in that game" (1961, p. 108).

Certain cautions are appropriate in studying Berne's system. First, as he himself points out, the very stereotype of the patterns is characteristic of neurotic behavior and not of the more flexible and mutually facilitative interactions between mature adults. Investigators may be tempted by the relative research convenience of a world whose inhabitants obligingly follow fixed patterns, as one sees in papers on marriage, but the assumption has many potential pitfalls. Second, the specific games described by Berne may be more useful as amusing illustrative sketches than as a new diagnostic system. There is little evidence of the reliability or functional necessity for such an extensive rogue's gallery. The very size of the catalogue makes it unwieldy. Nevertheless, the novelty of Berne's useful effort calls attentions to the dearth of terminology in academic and clinical psychology for the description of interpersonal transactions.

An interesting footnote to Levinger's "note" is that while he urged the "continued viability of the complementarity principle," he himself subsequently moved to the Parsons–Bales reformulation advocated by Tharp. In a paper on "Interpersonal Attraction and Agreement: A Study of Marriage Partners" (1966), Levinger and Breedlove distinguished between "social-emotional" and "task-oriented" sources of satisfaction in couples, by means of "a lengthy interview, conducted with husband and wife in separate rooms" (p. 368). The report made no reference to Parsons and Bales.

CLARIFICATION RECLARIFIED: IS EUTHANASIA INDICATED?

Although Tharp recommends the demise of both complementarity and similarity theories, they have bravely persisted, particularly the latter. A fairly recent version was the testing of the hypothesis that people will tend to choose dates "who are similar in social desirability" (Walster et al., 1966). The investigators staged a blind-date party on a college campus, combining boy and girl randomly, although all were carefully tested under the pretext of gathering data for computer matchings. The question was which combinations would prove sufficiently satisfying to lead to a second date. This study emerged with a serendipitous finding never previously tested by the experts which confirmed what might be dubbed the Playboy hypothesis rather than the similarity theory. As the authors reported, with some surprise: "Regardless of S's own attractiveness, by far the largest determinant of how much his partner was liked, how much he wanted to date the partner again, and how often he actually asked the partner out was simply how attractive the partner was. Personality measures . . . did not predict compatibility. The only important determinant of S's liking for his date was the date's physical attractiveness" (p. 508).

At the same time, the Parsonian "functionalist" position supported by Tharp also has persisted. One relevant and noteworthy study by Murrell and Stachowiak (1967) found that "the leadership pattern in the nonclinic families fits well with Parsons' (1955) description of family roles" (p. 271). At least equally as significant as the findings, however, are its new methods of study. In a county guidance center, tape recordings were made of family interactions as they participated in a number of assigned tasks and the frequencies of "who talked to whom" rather than verbal contents were counted. It should be noted that the researchers were psychologists working in a clinical setting and publishing in the *Journal of Abnormal Psychology*. This is indicative of a new trend in which family research was becoming more a part of psychology and less of sociology. Curiously, despite its successes, the Parsons theory had not brought a burgeoning of sociological work on the family. In fact, "The number of articles and research projects involving the family have declined in proportion to other pursuits," according to a published observation by the editor of *Sociology and Social Research* (Peterson, 1967). But, as the date indicates, this mystery moves us ahead of our own story.

MARITAL ROLE AND SOCIAL RANK

"Blue-Collar Families" is apparently not concerned with the similarity–complementarity issue, but it does produce a conclusion relevant to it. Professor Komarovsky asks what is essentially the second question raised earlier in our introduction: Is it possible to identify different types of families, with different types of husband–wife interaction? For her typology, she also departs from the Winch strategy and turns to the sociological characteristic of status, rather than to a psychological patterning. If we were to summarize her findings in terms of the conceptual Iron Maiden of similarity–complementarity language, it would have to be put that working class roles are complementary, in that there is a "traditional division of masculine and feminine tasks." Middle class marital roles show "similarity" in that they overlap to the extent that husband and wife "are troubled by the ambiguity of marriage roles." Thus, both similarity and complementarity explanations may be pertinent to different groups!

After reading the Komarovsky paper, however, one senses that this way of stating the case is not quite adequate. For instance, the term "complementarity" as applied to lower class spouses does not convey the considerable psychological distances that may exist between them (see, e. g., Grey, 1969, pp. 150–155). Nor is there any typology that can neatly convey this quality along with the other characteristics sketched by Dr. Komarovsky, apart from the very kind of description she provides. Terms like "authoritarianism" come to mind, but they offer too loose a fit for the task at hand, particularly in the light of the paper by Straus (1967), which is discussed below. Undoubtedly, complementarity research has been handicapped by limitations in currently available schema for thinking about personality phenomena.

Professor Komarovsky's paper also has implications for Parsons' theories about the family. Like him, she sees a relationship between behavior within the home and the total social circumstances within which the family functions. The point has been pursued even more explicitly in a study by Pearlin and Kohn (1966) which establishes connections between occupational roles and marital roles.

While Parsons' functionalism urges intimate acquaintance with the full range of interlocking life circumstances, his writings have often neglected such considerations in practice. A case in point is the very same Parsons–Bales formulation of American family patterns, which does not consider possible distinctions between class levels. That such a difference exists has been confirmed by a number of studies before and since Komarovsky (see, e. g., Grey, 1969). Particularly relevant here is the article by Straus (1967) on "The Influence of Sex of Child and Social Class on Instrumental and Expressive Family Roles in a Laboratory Setting." Part of the new trend toward direct observation of interaction, Straus' research uncovered class differences similar to those in the Komarovsky study. He also noted certain aspects of power structure not so apparent in her work. To quote part of Straus' conclusions:

> Finally, the paper examined the Parsons-Bales theory of instrumental and expressive role differentiation within the nuclear family, and the issue of the relative power of husband and wife in working and middle class families. The data show that, contrary to the Parsons-Bales theory, husbands tend to be predominant in both instrumental and expressive roles (particularly among middle class families). Although the husbands tended to be the key initiators of both instrumental and supportive acts, the data revealed that the working class husbands were relatively low in initiating all types of acts, whereas for the wives the class differences were minimal. Consequently, because of the relatively low role performance of working class husbands, the wives in this group were found to exercise more power relative to their husbands than was the case in the middle class families (p. 19).

The importance of precision in personality description is suggested by this statement. For instance, middle class husbands prove to exercise more real authority than do lower class men, despite a less authoritarian *manner*. One defect of the Parsons theory lies not in its general premises but in the vagueness attendant on its broad sweep (see, e.g., Scott, 1968). Thus, while its assertions of interrelatedness between family and society are substantiated, the specific predictions about family roles by Parsons and Bales prove more applicable to a particular social class, and also deficient in separating the appearance from the substance of power.

FROM COMPARISON OF INDIVIDUAL
PATTERNS TO FAMILY INTERACTION

Like Komarovsky, Handel has left behind the separate assessment of husbands and wives. He has moved to the orientation
of the second of our research questions. Even more than in the
previous essay, one can appreciate how radical a shift is involved in this new way of putting the matter. While the review-
er's concern is directed more toward psychological than sociological characteristics, its focus is very much on the interpersonal context rather than on individuals. For him, the transactional pattern that evolves among family members is distinctly
separable from their several personalities, and more pertinent
to the understanding and prediction of what happens to them.

How is it that the family pattern may be unpredictable or at
least different from the patterns of individual members? Consider that every individual has multiple potentialities not all of
which are conveniently elicited by any one test or battery of
tests. Similarly, varying facets of one's personality may be
evoked in various interpersonal settings. The particular style of
behavior will depend on whom one encounters and on their
mutual effects on each other. This should be even more true
for normal men, acting appropriately, than for disturbed people with rigid defensive systems. Secure people are aware of
social circumstances and role definitions as well as of their own
psychological needs. These considerations do not rule out underlying persistent tendencies in the character of any one human being. It merely asserts that such regularities do not
encompass the total personality. Thus the best predictions are
likely to be derived from observations drawn from the particular situation about which predictions are being attempted.

As Handel notes, this family interaction approach has been developed in the clinic—by psychoanalysts, psychologists, and
psychiatrists. In fact, one of his major points is to view with alarm
the relative inactivity of academic psychologists in this area:

> There can be little doubt that psychiatry now leads the way
> (although admittedly sometimes in collaboration with psycholo-

gists and other social scientists) in attempting to understand the family from a psychosocial point of view. If psychology as a discipline does not soon address itself more vigorously to this problem, the result may be that a generation hence psychologists will be devoting their time to trying to verify propositions originating in family psychiatry, just as in the field of personality study they have been significantly preoccupied with the merits of propositions originating in psychoanalysis (pp. 141–142).

One clear danger inherent in the clinical approach is that it may distort our understanding of family processes insofar as the results are derived from disturbed rather than normal samples. On the other hand, even such information can hardly be dismissed as valueless, particularly because it has already proven seminal in such instances as psychoanalysis. In various areas the clinical approach seems to have been more productive than the laboratory. The very frequency of this phenomenon makes one wonder wherein lies the strength of clinical research.

Were we to examine the history of the natural sciences, some might be surprised to discover that they include certain parallel experiences to the social sciences, at least in the matter of cross-fertilization between "pure" and "applied" aspects. The distinguished chemist and educator, James B. Conant (1947), suggests that we eschew "any false snobbery about the superiority of one activity over the other" (p. 35) for "the connection is a two-way street" (p. 36).

The practical arts at first run ahead of the sciences; only in very recent years have scientific discoveries affected practice to a greater extent than practice has affected science. Returning for a moment to the physical sciences, one may recall that the late Professor L. J. Henderson was fond of remarking that before 1850 the steam engine did more for science than science did for the steam engine (p. 36).

Those interested in pursuing this controversy about applied clinical research somewhat further might consult the recent and lively discussions by Bakan (1967) and Peterson (1968).

Returning to Handel's paper, it should be noted that the unabridged form contains a number of references to clinical research which are retained in the reprinted bibliography although excised from the text of the essay. Because space considerations required shortening this especially extensive paper, the most specialized clinical discussions were eliminated. The policy was to cut a few whole topics rather than single words, sentences, or even paragraphs, lest meanings be distorted inadvertently. The two omitted sections are "Family Structure as a Personality Component" and a summary of research on families of extremely pathological patients, "Family Communication and Schizophrenia."

Even with some deletion of clinical studies, Handel's survey provides clues to the particular strengths of good clinical research. For one thing, its methods more often are flexible and genuinely exploratory in the spirit urged by Bakan. Also the clinic patient's need for help makes him readier to expose himself to intimate scrutiny and radical manipulations. The practical urgencies of the clinician's task, the need for his sustained contact with patients, allow him to become intimately familiar with real persons in real social contexts. Actually, the clinician's role requires that he be an applied expert in small group process. It is precisely such skills and data that are more and more required by the increasingly sophisticated formulations of family research academicians.

Does the "Whole Family" Approach Have Clinical Validity?

Among the noteworthy features of Jackson's paper is his direct reference to a school of sociological thought, the Interactionists, as one of his theoretical sources. Clearly, the link between sociology and psychiatry in the family field has become a two-way communication, not merely a coincidental parallelism in an idea or two. While Jackson identifies the Interactionists (via Shibutani) quite explicitly, his discussion does speak of interlocking social systems in a manner reminiscent of Parsons. And it refers to interpersonal phenomena as Sullivan might have done, and to "present (observable) process" in the language of small group study. Not one but "many of the great theories of contemporary behavioral science . . . refer to 'interaction,' 'relationships,' etc.," he aptly observes. He is committed to the task of translating these astute but vaguely defined ideas into operational procedures, applicable to identifiable events, to what some call the "clinical data." Much of the impetus derives from the great promise shown by conjoint family therapy. The clinical illustration of a mutually reinforcing husband-wife conflict moves our attention from strained constructs to what begin to sound like a flesh-and-blood couple.

The subsequent discussion makes it quite evident that the shift from a primary focus on separate individuals to the patient as part of a system is not universally hailed as a great advance in the clinical world. Any notion of "clinical thought" as a single monolithic orientation, free from controversy, is dispelled by the acrimonious interchange. Jackson is prompt to identify the enemy forces as "psychoanalytic," thereby touching on another conflict still active in the psychiatric world (see, e. g., Grey, 1969). His characterization of psychoanalysis, however, expresses some personal bias about that school rather than an objective picture of the facts.

It is quite true that classical psychoanalysis was focused on persons rather than on systems. An atomistic approach was generally characteristic of nineteenth-century science. It also is true that many conservative psychoanalysts continue in that orientation, manifesting an apparent death wish in their adherence to outmoded formulations. But it is equally true that still other psychoanalysts have pioneered the new whole family approach, notably those cited by Handel in that section of his review (in this volume) entitled "The Emergence of the Problem." The family system approach hardly would have been opposed by the neo-Freudian Sullivan, who long regarded psychiatry as "much the same field which is studied by social psychology because scientific psychiatry has to be defined as the study of interpersonal relations" (1948).

CLINICAL VALIDITY DEMONSTRATED: FAMILY SYSTEM EFFECTS VERSUS DRUG EFFECTS

In this age, when tranquilizers have "revolutionized the management of psychotic patients" (Joint Commission on Mental Illness, 1961, p. 37), what more impressive evidence can be asked for the "reality" of the family as a social system than that it has effects equivalent in potency to psychopharmaceuticals? The study by Cohen et al. (1968) seems to provide the kind of facts demanded by Dr. Epstein in his criticism of Jackson, presented immediately before this paper. It also proposes a principle of role "consonance" or complementarity for more explicit understanding of how the family system works. The idea is quite reminiscent of Winch or even of the Interactionist view that "the self arises out of social interaction" (Sarbin, 1954, p. 238). At the same time, the process is spelled out more concretely, in terms of specific provocative behavior amenable to direct observation.

Despite its neatness, an important reservation to be kept in mind about the study is the inconclusiveness of its evidence. Several objective measures of the conventional verbal self-report variety proved less informative than the ratings of social behavior gleaned from relatives who served as participant observers. My guess is that interaction data available to the observers were more directly relevant, more valid, than tests which are not based on actual behavior in the family setting. Many psychometric studies in this area seem to overlook the consideration that objectivity in itself does not overcome irrelevance or poor quality in the basic data. At the same time, it must also be recognized that the observation reports in this research fell distinctly short of the ideal. That is, they did not include a detailed record of the postulated interactions by procedures of known reliability.

Had it been feasible to post observers in the home, with systematic observation schedules, some of these deficiencies might have been overcome. Obviously, such a procedure would involve many practical difficulties. What other strategies might be relevant? The research task undertaken by Cohen et al. was to determine how the interpersonal system of the family affects the behavior of a given member. This suggests observations of how the subjects behave while living with their families as compared with their behavior when apart from them. Thus, out of the series of investigations a new question has emerged, the third one listed in the introductory section. How is the response style of an individual affected by the presence or absence of other family members? A relevant design might be to observe each patient group while living at home for an adequate time period and then, over an equally long span, in another environment. This requires a standardized "away from home" setting. Also the chronological order of the two phases would have to be varied among the patients to control for sequence effects.

Here again, the practical considerations become rather formidable. To answer the question of family influence and yet circumvent these obstacles, in 1951 Strodtbeck had devised the Revealed Difference Technique (RDT). Essentially, it is a procedure in which family members (usually husband and wife) answer set questions individually and then come together to resolve any differences. This device does not adequately measure long-term effects but its relative convenience has brought the basic design into increasing favor in recent years. The study by Straus (1967), described earlier, is an example of this kind of research technique.

Assessing the Part from the System

The Farina–Holzberg investigation (1968) offers a readily identifiable methodological improvement over the drug study just discussed. For exploration of family interactions it obtains taped records whose data are scored by methods of known reliability. These authors are not the first, of course, to study interaction directly to treat the style in which people speak to each other as more noteworthy than the contents of what they say. Similar procedures are to be found in such recent researches as the already cited papers by Murrell and Stachowiak (1967), by Straus (1967), and also in projects by Morris and Wynne (1965), Palombo et al. (1967), Dorfman (1968), Gassner and Murray (1969), among others. Several, like the Farina and Holzberg paper, also use a comparison of persons observed apart and together, following the Strodtbeck device.

On first consideration, the results reported by Farina and Holzberg may appear informative without being suprising. As they point out, previous literature concurs with their finding that husband and wife pairs who display greater mutual conflict have more seriously disturbed sons. Certain discrepancies between their findings and earlier work again highlight the importance of technical problems like how to measure "dominance." What is most striking, however, is that more effective discrimination is possible between prognostically "good" and "poor" sons by scrutinizing the interaction between their parents than by studying the patients' own responses to them! It moves marital group process research to a position dramatically opposite from our point of departure, the 1954 Winch paper. Formulations of that vintage, whether they favored complementarity or similarity, attempted a portrait of the household *Gestalt* from separate scrutiny of man and wife. By contrast, the present essay suggests that for certain purposes one need study only the groups together.

One might even take this principle a step beyond and speculate whether an absent family member might be diagnosed from the behavior of those present, particularly if the available sample included key figures like the parents. Just such a series of studies has been done, in fact, by Palombo et al. (1967), and by Morris and Wynne (1965), who concluded, "We find that different forms or styles of parental communication . . . can be discriminated from one another and that these differen-

tiations can be used to predict accurately the psychiatric diagnosis and form of thinking and affect in the offspring" (1965,
pp. 19–20).

One cannot help but wonder why the husband–wife interactions yielded more distinct results than those involving the
patient himself. Could it have been that the son's separation
from his mother and father by his hospital stay had weakened
temporarily certain response patterns in him, although not in
the parents who remained together? Could it have been that
the son's social role as patient (see, e.g., Goffman, 1961)
made him more self-critical and subdued in the presence of his
parents than he had been previously? As they become more
precise, interaction studies will have to take increasing account
of the longer time spans and wider social milieux in which they
are set.

Where Do We Go from Here?

As used by Bauman et al. (1967), the Interaction Testing
approach can be recognized as still another adaptation of the
subjects-apart-versus-together strategy associated with Strodtbeck. Its particular advantages lie in convenience (by
comparison with the methods of Farina and Holzberg, for
instance) and in the availability of intelligence measures as
clear-cut criteria by which to estimate fluctuations in the level
of performance. Among its limitations is the fact that a far
wider range of behavior must be sampled for a full picture of
how husbands and wives interact. It is conceivable, however,
that the same strategy can be extended to such other activities.

The relative convenience of Interaction Testing is not to be
dismissed as trivial. As is evident from the earlier history of
marriage research, it was their convenience that led to so wide
a use of questionnaires. Perhaps the parallel virtues of interaction testing methods will bring more groups of normal subjects
into the range of accessibility. Then the present overconcentra-
tion on clinical subjects can be rectified. Wider use undoubted-

ly will bring out shortcomings in this approach which are not yet evident.

One improvement that might be considered is the possibility of registering *sequences* of interaction as well as simply the frequencies with which certain behaviors occur. Following sequences might give richer clues to the processes by which marital partners engage in, say, collaboration, and a more profound picture of the quality of the relationship. Consider the following interchange:

Wife: Why has Junior been doing so poorly in school lately?
   (A solicitation of assistance)
Husband: He's been caught up in the baseball season. Maybe he hasn't been giving it enough time.
   (A response offering help)
Wife: No. He spends as much time at homework as he ever has.
   (Rejection of the help as useless)
Husband: Maybe the new science course has him discouraged. He never cared much about science.
   (Another move to help)
Wife: I don't know. He's doing as well in science as he does in English.
   (Another rejection)
Husband: Well, you've got me. I just don't know.
   (Withdrawal from effort to help)
Wife: I think I'll talk to his teacher.
   (Acceptance of the withdrawal and of husband's inability to help)

From the ready way in which both husband and wife abandon the collaboration, an observer might suspect that neither is very strongly motivated to achieve it. Perhaps the wife wishes to feel superior in this domain and the husband is happy to leave the responsibility to her. From examination of the frequency with which any whole sequence occurs, the specific issues which evoke it, the varying roles adopted by husband

and wife, even the preceding events, a more refined portrait of the marriage might be developed. The task of adapting such sequence analysis to interaction testing does not seem impossible. Thus content and sequence might enrich understanding of the relationship and provide a more sensitive measure of any changes in it. These kinds of data often are used by clinicians with varying degrees of awareness. The reader may recognize sequence analysis as one of the features of Berne's "game" theory.

Berne has not extended this idea to the detection of fresh trends in the relationship between man and wife, but herein lies another important possibility. Married couples might be re-exposed to interaction testing over a period of time to plot trends in the evolution of their relationship or the effects of psychotherapy. Considered in this way, the study of immediate interactions can contribute to an understanding of how a family develops over the whole span of its history, from courtship to termination in death or voluntary separation. If this more ambitious task is undertaken by researchers, some new questions can be anticipated for addition to our initial list. For instance, is it possible, from spaced studies of family interaction, to distinguish types of marriage relationships, each with its own characteristic interpersonal stages over time?

An affirmative answer would open the path to using earlier stages for making predictions about later ones. A mutually contributory link might be forged between interaction studies and the developmental approach to family life. (For a review of the latter field, see Hill, 1964) With sufficiently accurate diagnostic procedures, it might become feasible to have "marriage check-ups" allowing for experts to intervene helpfully before difficulties become irremediably severe. The contemplation of a promising new tool for investigation can inspire many encouraging speculations, which is one good reason for choosing an essay on the subject as the terminal paper in a collection.

At the same time, it is evident that no matter how skillfully the interaction between partners is measured, interpersonal transactions between them are not the sole determinant of the history of an enduring relationship. Many events and circumstances combine to affect its course, including wars, economic cycles, new technology, political events, and the fortunate or unfortunate accidents of daily life.

A SUMMARY OVERVIEW

We have moved only a short distance beyond the beginning of an explicit understanding of the nature of family interaction. Perhaps the major discovery is one that has grown out of psychodynamic clinical study, confirmed by more recent formal research. It is that the relationship between husband and wife, and their children, constitutes an interpersonal system not predictable simply from information about individual family members. The papers by Handel, Jackson, and Farina and Holzberg make this point in their various ways.

When families are compared on the basis of psychological criteria, as in the essays cited above, or on the basis of sociological variables, as in the social class comparison by Komarovsky, typical kinds of interaction between husband and wife are seen to be associated with the typologies. Broadly stated, more discord characterizes the interaction between spouses with emotionally disturbed offspring, and more separation of roles and attitudes is found at lower socioeconomic levels. There also is evidence of a kind of family homeostasis, a tendency for members to preserve familiar patterns, as shown by Cohen et al., although this evidence is more extensive for disturbed families than for the general population.

While a number of obvious considerations, as well as current personality theories, suggest that normal groups are different from the emotionally disturbed in such matters as flexibility of behavior, the question has not yet been investigated adequately. This is partly the consequence of a shift in the professional identity of those doing marital research. Where earlier studies were undertaken primarily by sociologists using questionnaires to examine normal groups (often college students), recent trends are toward increasingly sophisticated direct observation more readily accomplished with clinical populations.

The knowledge accumulated thus far is modest, but it also includes useful information about pitfalls to be avoided. For instance, the nature of interpersonal processes is seen as far too complex to be explained under mutually exclusive simplistic labels like "similarity" or "complementarity." Pioneer efforts by Winch, and critical evaluations by experts like Levinger and Tharp all help to make that evident. Not the least achievement of marriage research has been the progressive development of more flexible and sensitive research devices, such as the promising strategy of Interaction Testing (Bauman et al., 1967), for further exploration of these complex interpersonal transactions. Hopefully, the new methods and their successors will contribute to the improvement of existing theories of interpersonal relations by bridging the gap between inspired observation and systematic verification.

REFERENCES

Ackerman, N. W. The diagnosis of neurotic marital interaction. *Social Casework, 1954, 35:* 4.

Bakan, D. *On method; toward a reconstruction of psychological investigation.* San Francisco: Jossey-Bass Inc., 1967.

Bales, R. F. The equilibrium problem in small groups. In T. Parsons, R. F. Bales, and E. A. Shils. *Working papers in the theory of action.* New York: The Free Press, 1953.

Bardis, P. D. Family forms and variations historically considered. In H. T. Christensen (ed.) *Handbook of marriage and the family.* Chicago: Rand McNally, 1964.

Bateson, G., and M. Mead. *Balinese character; A photographic analysis.* New York: New York Academy of Science, 1942.

*Bauman, G., M., Roman, J. Borello, and B. Meltzer. Interaction testing in the measurement of marital intelligence. *Journal of Abnormal Psychology, 1967, 72,* 489–495.

Berne, E. *Games people play.* New York: Grove Press, 1964.

Berne, E. *Transactional analysis in psychotherapy.* New York: Grove Press, 1961.

Asterisk (*) denotes article included in this volume.

Burchinal, L. G. The premarital dyad and love involvement. In H. T. Christensen (ed.) *Handbook of marriage and the family.* Chicago: Rand McNally, 1964.

Burgess, E. W. The family as a unity of interacting personalities. *Family,* 1926, *7,* 3–9.

Burgess, E. W., and P. Wallin. *Engagement and marriage.* New York: Lippincott, 1953.

Burgess, E. W., and L. Cottrell. *Predicting success or failure in marriage.* Englewood Cliffs, N. J.: Prentice-Hall, 1939.

Christensen, H. T. Development of the family field of study. In H. T. Christensen (ed.) *Handbook of marriage and the family.* Chicago: Rand McNally, 1964.

*Cohen, M., N. Freedman, D. M. Engelhardt, and R. A. Margolis. Family interaction patterns, drug treatment and change in social aggression. *Archives of General Psychiatry,* 1968, *19,* 50–56.

Conant, J. B. *On understanding science.* New Haven: Yale University Press, 1947.

Cooley, C. H. *Social organization.* New York: Scribner's, 1909.

Cottrell, L. S., and N. N. Foote. Sullivan's contribution to social psychology. In P. Mullahy (ed.), *The contributions of Harry Stack Sullivan: A symposium on interpersonal theory in psychiatry and social science.* New York: Hermitage House, 1952.

Deutsch, M. Field theory in social psychology. In G. Lindzey (ed.), *Handbook of social psychology.* Reading, Mass.: Addison-Wesley, 1954.

Dewey, J. *Human nature and conduct.* New York: Modern Library, 1930.

Dorfman, E. Content-free study of marital resemblances in group therapy. *Journal of Abnormal Psychology,* 1968, *73,* 78–80.

*Epstein, N. B. Discussion of "The Individual and the Larger Contexts." *Family Process,* 1967, 151–152.

*Farina, A., and J. D. Holzberg. Interaction patterns of parents and hospitalized sons diagnosed as schizophrenic or nonschizophrenic. *Journal of Abnormal Psychology,* 1968, *73,* 114–118.

Festinger, L. *A theory of cognitive dissonance.* Stanford: Stanford University Press, 1957.

Foote, N. N. Love. *Psychiatry,* 1953, *16,* 245–251.

Freud, S. *An outline of psychoanalysis.* New York: Norton, 1949.

Fromm, E. *Escape from freedom.* New York: Rinehart, 1941.

Gassner, S., and E. J. Murray. Dominance and conflict in the interactions between parents of normal and neurotic children. *Journal of Abnormal Psychology,* 1969, *74,* 33–41.

Gerard, H. B., and N. Miller. Group dynamics. In P. R. Farnsworth, O. McNemar, and I. McNemar (eds.), *Annual Review of Psychology,* Vol. 18, Palo Alto, Calif.: Annual Reviews, Inc., 1967.

Goffman, E. *Asylums.* New York: Doubleday, 1961.

Goode, W. J. *World revolution and family patterns.* New York: The Free Press, 1963.

Grey, A. (ed.), *Class and personality in society.* New York: Atherton Press, 1969.

Hall, E. T. *The silent language.* New York: Doubleday, 1959.

*Handel, G. Psychological study of whole families. *Psychological Bulletin,* 1965, *63,* 19–41.

Heider, F. *The psychology of interpersonal relations.* New York: Wiley, 1958.

Hill, R. The developmental approach. In H. T. Christensen (ed.), *Handbook of marriage and the family.* Chicago: Rand McNally, 1964.

Hill, R., and D. A. Hansen. The identification of conceptual frameworks utilized in family study. *Marriage and Family Living,* 1960, *22,* 299–311.

Hinsie, L. E., and J. Shatzky. *Psychiatric dictionary.* New York: Oxford University Press, 1940.

Inkeles, A. Personality and social structure. In R. K. Merton, L. Broom, and L. S. Cottrell, Jr. (eds.) *Sociology today.* New York: Basic Books, 1959.

*Jackson, D. The individual and the larger contexts. *Family Process,* 1967, *6,* 139–147.

*Jackson, D. D. Reply to discussion of "The Individual and the Larger Contexts." *Family Process,* 1967, 154.

James, W. *Psychology.* New York: Holt, 1892.

Joint Commission on Mental Illness and Health. *Action for mental health.* New York: Basic Books, 1961.

Kelley, H. H., and J. W. Thibaut. Experimental studies of group problem solving and process. In G. Lindzey (ed.), *Handbook of social psychology.* Reading, Mass.: Addison-Wesley, 1954.

Kleinmuntz, B. *Personality measurement; an introduction.* Homewood, Ill.: Dorsey Press, 1967.

Klineberg, O. Discussion. In P. Mullahy (ed.), *The contributions of Harry Stack Sullivan; A symposium on interpersonal theory in psychiatry and social science.* New York: Hermitage House, 1952.

*Komarovsky, M. Blue-collar families. *Columbia University Forum,* 1964, VII, 29–32.

Lambert, W. W. Stimulus-response contiguity and reinforcement theory in social psychology. In G. Lindzey (ed.) *Handbook of social psychology.* Reading, Mass.: Addison-Wesley, 1954.

Lantz, H. R., E. C. Snyder, M. Britton, and R. Schmitt. Pre-industrial patterns in the colonial family in America: A content analysis of colonial magazines. *American Sociological Review,* 1968, *33,* 413–426.

Levinger, G., and J. Breedlove. Interpersonal attraction and agreement: A study of marriage partners. *Journal of Personality and Social Psychology,* 1966, *3,* 367–372.

*Levinger, G. Note on need complementarity in marriage. *Psychological Bulletin,* 1964, *61,* 153–157.

Lindzey, G., and D. Byrne. Measurement of social choice and interpersonal attractiveness. In G. Lindzey and E. Aronson (eds.), *The handbook of social psychology, 2d ed.,* Vol. II. Reading, Mass.: Addison-Wesley, 1969.

Lindzey, G. (ed.), *Handbook of social psychology* (2 vols.). Reading, Mass.: Addison-Wesley, 1954.

Lorge, I., D. Fox, J. Davitz, and M. Brenner. A survey of studies contrasting the quality of group performances and individual performance, 1920–1957. *Psychological Bulletin,* 1958, *55,* 337–372.

Marlowe, D., and K. J. Gergen. Personality and social interaction. In G. Lindzey and E. Aronson (eds.), *The handbook of social psychology,* 2d ed., Vol. III. Reading Mass.: Addison-Wesley, 1969.

Masters, W. H., and V. E. Johnson. *Human sexual response.* Boston: Little, Brown, 1966.

Mead, G. H. *Mind, self and society.* Chicago: University of Chicago Press, 1934.

Mogey, J. Family and community in urban-industrial societies. In H. T.

Christensen (ed.), *Handbook of marriage and the family.* Chicago: Rand McNally, 1964.

Morris, G. O., and L. C. Wynne. Schizophrenic offspring and parental styles of communication. *Psychiatry,* 1965, *28,* 19–44.

Murdock, G. P. *Social structure.* New York: Hacmillan, 1949.

Murphy, G., and E. Cattell. Sullivan and field theory. In P. Mullahy (ed.), *The contributions of Harry Stack Sullivan: a symposium on interpersonal theory in psychiatry and social science.* New York: Hermitage House, 1952.

Murrell, S. A., and J. G. Stachowiak. Consistency, rigidity and power in the interaction patterns of clinic and nonclinic families. *Journal of abnormal psychology,* 1967, *72,* 265–272.

Newcomb, T. M. *The acquaintance process.* New York: Holt, Rinehart and Winston, 1961.

Newcomb, T. M. Individual systems of orientation. In S. Koch (ed.), *Psychology: a study of a science.* Vol. 3, New York: McGraw-Hill, 1959.

Newcomb, T. M. The prediction of interpersonal attraction. *American Psychologist,* 1956, *11,* 575–586.

Nye, F. I., and A. E. Bayer. Some recent trends in family research. *Social Forces,* 1963, *41,* 290–301.

Oberndorf, C. P. Psychoanalysis of married couples. *Psychoanalytic Review,* 1938, *25,* 453–457.

Palombo, S. R., J. Merrifield, W. Weigert, G. O. Morris, and L. C. Wynne. Recognition of parents of schizophrenics from excerpts of family therapy interviews. *Psychiatry,* 1967, *30,* 405–412.

Parsons, T. Social structure and the development on personality—Freud's contribution to the integration of psychology and sociology. *Psychiatry,* 1958, *21,* 321–340.

Parsons, T., and R. F. Bales. *Family, socialization and interaction process.* New York: The Free Press, 1955.

Parsons, T., and E. A. Shils (eds.), *Toward a general theory of action.* Cambridge, Mass.: Harvard University Press, 1951.

Pearlin, L. I., and M. L. Kohn. Social class, occupation and parental values: a cross-national study. *American Sociological Review,* 1966, *31,* 466–479.

Peterson, D. *The clinical study of social behavior.* New York: Appleton-Century-Crofts, 1968.

Peterson, J. A. Preface. *Sociology and Social Research,* 1967, *52,* 5–6.

Potter, D. M. *People of plenty: Economic abundance and the American character.* Chicago: University of Chicago Press, 1954.

Sarbin, T. R. Role theory. In G. Lindzey (ed.), *Handbook of social psychology.* Reading, Mass.: Addison-Wesley, 1954.

Scott, J. F., in Review symposium: Talcott Parsons, *Socialological theory and modern society. American Sociological Review,* 1968, *33,* pp. 453–456.

Shepherd, C. R. *Small groups: Some sociological perspectives.* San Francisco: Chandler Publishing Co., 1964.

Straus, M. A. The influence of sex of child and social class on instrumental and expressive family roles in a laboratory setting. *Sociology and Social Research,* 1967, *52,* 7–21.

Strodtbeck, F. L. The family as a three-person group. *American Sociological Review,* 1954, *19,* 23–29.

Strodtbeck, F. L. Husband-wife interaction over revealed differences. *American Sociological Review,* 1951, *16,* 468–473.

Stryker, S. The interactional and situational approaches. In H. T. Christensen (ed.), *Handbook of marriage and the family.* Chicago: Rand McNally, 1964.

Sullivan, H. S. *Conceptions of modern psychiatry.* Washington, D.C.: William Alanson White Psychiatric Foundation, 1947.

Sullivan, H. S. Towards a psychiatry of peoples. *Psychiatry,* 1948, *11,* 105–116.

*Tharp, R. G. Psychological patterning in marriage. *Psychological Bulletin,* 1963, *60,* 97–117.

*Tharp, R. G. Reply to Levinger's note. *Psychological Bulletin,* 1964, *61,* 158–160.

Thomas, W. I. The behavior pattern and the situation. *Publications of the American Sociological Society,* 1927, *22,* 1–13.

Tönnies, F. *Community and society.* East Lansing, Mich.: The Michigan State University Press, 1957.

*Vassiliou, G. Discussion of "The Individual and the Larger Contexts." *Family Process,* 1967, 148–151.

Vaughan, T. R., and L. T. Reynolds. The sociology of symbolic interactionism. *American Sociologist,* 1968, *3,* 208–214.

Walster, E., V. Aronson, D. Abrahams, and L. Rottmann. Importance of physical attractiveness in dating behavior. *Journal of personality and social psychology.* 1966, *4,* 508–516.

Winch, R. F. *The modern family* (rev. ed.). New York: Holt, Rinehart and Winston, 1963.

Winch, R. F. The theory of complementary needs in mate-selection: Final results on the test of general hypotheses. *American Sociological Review,* 1955, *20,* 552–555.

*Winch, R. F., T. Ktsanes, and V. Ktsanes. The theory of complementary needs in mate-selection: An analytic and descriptive study. *American Sociological Review,* 1954, *19,* 241–249.

*Wynne, L. C. Discussion of "The Individual and the Larger Contexts." *Family Process,* 1967, 153 154.

Zelditch, M., Jr. Cross-cultural analysis of family structure. In H. T. Christensen (ed.), *Handbook of marriage and the family.* Chicago: Rand McNally, 1964.

Zelditch, M., Jr. Role differentiation in the nuclear family: A comparative study. In T. Parsons and R. F. Bales, with J. Olds, M. Zelditch, Jr., and P. Slater, *Family, socialization and interaction process.* New York: The Free Press, 1955, pp. 307–352.

Zicklin, G. A conversation concerning face-to-face interaction. *Psychiatry,* 1968, *31,* 236–249.

1

The Theory of Complementary Needs in Mate-Selection: An Analytic and Descriptive Study

ROBERT F. WINCH
THOMAS KTSANES
VIRGINIA KTSANES

In a sense, motives are abstractions from observed continuities in behavior. Prediction is a test of the conceptual worth of a motivational scheme. We reason that if the motivational pattern of an individual can be adequately described, then it should be possible to make two kinds of predictions: (a) the motivational patterns of persons with whom the first person will seek to interact, and (b) how he will behave with, and hence influence, persons with various kinds of motivational patterns.

In its general form (a) leads to a theory of selective interaction, of which the theory of complementary needs in mate-selection is a special case. This is the specific implication of the theory which we have undertaken to investigate. We have stated only one broad implication of (b) and have not undertaken any study along this line.[1]

From *American Sociological Review*, Vol. 19, No. 3, June 1954, pp. 241–248. This investigation was supported in part by a research grant (MH 439) from the National Institute of Mental Heath, United States Public Health Service, and in part by a grant from the Graduate School of Northwestern University.

THE THEORY OF COMPLEMENTARY NEEDS

The theory of motivation used in this study is a modified and simplified version of the Murray need schema.[2] Since the theory of motivation is general, it can subsume all human behavior, including such behavior as is involved in the interactional processes of courtship and mate-selection. If the theory is correct, it should be able to explain a considerable proportion of the variance in mate-selection. The theory of complementary needs in mate-selection is a specific application of the general motivational theory plus its implications for selective interaction in mate-selection.[3]

The theory proceeds from the observation that "love" is regarded as the *sine qua non* of marriage in middle-class America. For the purpose of this study "love" is defined as the experience of deriving gratification for important psychic needs from a peer-age person of the opposite sex, or the expectation of deriving such gratification.[4]

The basic hypothesis of the theory of complementary needs in mate-selection is that in mate-selection each individual seeks within his or her field of eligibles[5] for that person who gives the greatest promise of providing him or her with maximum need-gratification. It is not assumed that this process is totally or even largely conscious. For the present we leave the level of consciousness unspecified and a subject for investigation. We should anticipate, however, that the level of awareness of this process would vary from one person to another, and that persons who have relatively clear perception of their psychic processes would fall near the "totally aware" end of the continuum.

It follows from the general motivational theory that both the person to whom one is attracted, and the one being attracted, will be registering in behavior their own need-patterns. Then a second hypothesis follows from the first—that the need-pattern of *B*, the second person or the one to whom the first is attracted, will be *complementary* rather than *similar* to the need-pattern of *A*, the first person.

The latter is the hypothesis which this study is designed to test directly. Our reasoning is based on the postulate that as B acts out B's own need-pattern, B's resulting behavior will be a greater source of gratification to A than will be the case with the behavior of C, who is psychically similar to A. And reciprocally, A's behavior will be a greater source of gratification to B than will be the behavior of some other person who is psychically more similar to B.

Let us note some obvious and highly oversimplified examples. If A is highly ascendant, we should expect A to be more attracted maritally to B who is submissive than to C who, like A, is ascendant. If A is somewhat sadistic, we should expect A to be more attracted maritally to B who is somewhat masochistic than to C who is sadistic. If A is a succorant person, we should expect A to be attracted to nurturant B rather than to succorant C.[6] And in each of these cases B should be reciprocally attracted to A.

Perhaps it will facilitate communication if we offer an example in more conventional psychological language rather than in the specialized need terminology. Let us consider the hypothetical case of a passive-dependent male who, consciously or unconsciously, recognized and accepts this disposition in himself. We should hypothesize that the man would seek out a nurturant, maternal woman. If, however, he should reject his own need-pattern, we should expect the man to seek a very dependent "clinging vine." In the latter case the woman might find gratification in the man's behavior resulting from his compensatory defenses.[7]

NEED

It is now in order to explain the terms "need" and "complementary." We conceive of "need" as a goal-oriented drive, native or learned, which, as Murry says, "organizes perception, apperception, intellection, conation, and action in such a way as to transform in a certain direction an existing, unsatisfying situation."[8] Of course the goal need not be a material object, but any state of affairs which the individual senses would be more gratifying than the "existing, unsatisfying situation."

To test our hypothesis it is necessary to have some classification of needs (and some procedure for observing them. We begin by assuming that there is no one "correct" classification of needs.) Rather, one's research problem, and more specifically the kinds of behavior involved, should influence the needs posited and their definitions. This study employs an abridged and amended version of the classification set forth by H. A. Murray and associates in the work previously cited.[9]

In conceptualizing our study we felt that it would be contrary to common observation and experience if we were to postulate perfectly general needs, such as dominance, recognition, and the like. Rather it appeared necessary to take account of the level of awareness and expression and of the expected locus of gratification (or situation).

Although Freudian psychology specifically denotes three kinds or levels of consciousness (conscious, preconscious, and unconscious), Freud and others have remarked that this threefold classification is a heuristic device and that they really think of consciousness as a continuum with an unlimited number of levels of awareness from the most deeply repressed unconsciousness to completely verbalizable consciousness. Avenues of expression are proliferated, moreover, through the numerous mechanisms of defense. In an effort to keep our conceptual (and hence operational) schema as simple as possible, we posited only two levels—overt and covert. We accepted the overt–covert dichotomy as the most workable compromise with the Freudian view of psychic complexity.

Similarly, the recognition that to a considerable degree behavior is situation-specific can lead to the postulation of a classification containing an unlimited number of situations. Our prime concern is with marital situations. Accordingly, we chose the simplest classification: (*a*) within the marriage, and (*b*) all other situations.

Where feasible, therefore, we double-dichotomized our need

variables. For example, we posited overt dominance both within and outside the marriage and covert dominance both within and outside. We refer to dichotomized and double-dichotomized variables as subvariables. The application of these dichotomies made our 15 variables (*cf.* n. 9 above) into 44 subvariables.

COMPLEMENTARINESS

When two persons, *A* and *B*, are interacting, we consider the resulting gratifications of both to be "complementary" if one of the following conditions is satisfied: (1) the need or needs in *A* which are being gratified are *different in kind* from the need or needs being gratified in *B*; or (2) the need or needs in *A* which are being gratified are *very different in intensity* from the same needs in *B* which are also being gratified.

"An example of (1) is found in the case of a person desirous of attention and recognition [need recognition] who finds gratification in relationship with a person who tends to bestow admiration on the former [need deference]. Alternative (2) is illustrated in the interaction between a person who wants others to do his bidding [high need dominance] and one lacking the ability to handle his environment who is looking for someone to tell him what to do [low need dominance]. It will be recognized that this definition of complementariness embraces two forms of heterogamy."[10]

QUALIFICATIONS

Since the theory of complementary needs asserts that mate-selection is based on the psychic makeup of the individuals engaging in mutual choices and asserts further that the bases of the choices may be unconscious, it follows that the theory should be presumed to operate only where marriage partners are chosen voluntarily and mutually. In other words, it is not to be expected that the theory would be operative in a setting

where marriages are arranged (as by parents, marriage bro-
kers, or others). Both man and woman should have some
choice in the matter, moreover, even though the discretion
excercised be no more than the negative right to reject a
proposal for marriage to someone perceived as unsuitable.

For choice to exist, furthermore, each individual must have
a field of potential mates. Here we note the relevance of a
considerable number of studies which concur in concluding
that American marriages are homogamous. At first, it might
appear that these studies would contradict the theory of complementary needs in mate-selection. Where homogamy has
been conclusively shown, however, it has pertained to such
social characteristics as race, religion, educational level, and
social class. (We may regard the studies showing residential
propinquity of marriage partners as reporting homogamy in a
spatial sense.)[11] Rather than interpret these studies as contradictory to our theory, we regard them as not bearing directly on
motivational variables and instead as denoting a series of variables which serve to define and delimit for each individual a
set of marriageable persons. This set of marriageable persons is
designated by the term "field of eligibles."

These qualifications are incorporated into the theory in the
following way. The practice of the voluntary and mutual choice
of spouses means simply that mate selection occurs only between people who are acquainted with each other. The principle of homogamy with respect to social characteristics means
that those who are acquainted tend to be similar with respect
to these characteristics. From the consequently delimited field
of eligibles it is hypothesized that each person tends to select as
a spouse that person whom the first person perceives as giving
the greatest promise of providing himself or herself with need-
gratification.[12]

PROCEDURE

Our general procedure for a series of analyses in process
involves ratings by two or more judges on the basis of one or

more of three personal documents: (1) an interview structured to elicit evidence on these needs, called by us a "need-interview"; (2) a case-history interview; and (3) an eight-card thematic apperception test. Only one analysis has been completed thus far. Ktsanes and Ktsanes have performed what is in effect a content-analysis of the need-interviews. They have analyzed each subject's response to each question, have decided to which need or needs it relates, and have assigned ratings on a five-point basis to the reponses. The final rating given by each of these two raters to each subject on each subvariable was the arithmetic mean of ratings given to the individual responses. The mean of the two raters' final ratings was taken as the final datum for this analysis.[13]

THE SAMPLE

The subjects involved consist of a reasonably random sample of 25 native-born persons who were undergraduate students in selected schools at Northwestern University in 1950 and their spouses, or a total of 50 persons.[14] Restrictions were imposed on the sampling process so as to maximize homogeneity with repect to socioeconomic status, religion, race, age, etc.[15] In addition, all couples had been married less than two years and were childless. The purpose of the latter restrictions was to minimize the effect of marital interaction and thus to keep the personalities of our subjects as similar as possible to their patterns at the time of selecting their spouses.

Strictly speaking, therefore, the population consists of all married couples at Northwestern University with the characteristics specified above. It is plausible but not demonstrable that findings based on this sample may be generally valid for young American urban middle class "majority" couples with university training. Once the procedure and findings are clearly specified for the population sampled, determination of the range of generalizability becomes a question for further research.

RESULTS

The basic test of our hypothesis rests upon what we call an "interspousal correlation." That is, we run a product-moment correlation on normalized mean ratings between the husbands on sub variable X and their respective wives on subvariable Y. A concrete example is the correlation between the husbands' overt nurturance within the marriage and their respective wives' covert succorance within.

With 44 subvariables it is possible to compute 1,936 inter-spousal correlations. Out of this total we hypothesized the signs of 388 on the basis of the theory of complementary needs. For example, we hypothesized that selected nurturance-succorance correlations would be positive and that selected nurturance–nurturance correlations would be negative. In accordance with the two kinds of complementariness noted above, we hypothesized: (1) that 344 interspousal correlations, each of which involved two different needs or traits, would be positive; and (2) that 44 interspousal correlations involving the same need or trait would be negative. We should regard the evidence as supporting the general statement of the theory of complementary needs in mate-selection if the number of correlations which were significant in the hypothesized direction should exceed the number we might expect to occur by chance. Since our hypothesis involved the designation of the sign of the correlation, it was appropriate to use a one-tailed test of significance.

Table 1 lists the pairs of variables involved in the 344 two-variable interspousal correlations, which were hypothesized to be positive. Table 2 lists the 44 one-variable interspousal correlations, which were hypothesized to be negative. Table 3 summarized the totals of Tables 1 and 2.

Although it is clear from Table 4 that the data do not reveal anything like perfect results, it is equally clear that they diverge so much from chance in the direction hypothesized that the probability of the correctness of the null hypothesis is virtually infinitesimal. Thus it appears that persons like our subjects tend to select mates whose needs are complementary rather than similar to their own.[16]

PLANS FOR FURTHER ANALYSES

Table 4 presents a test of the general theory of complementary needs, and it is clear that the theory passes the test. We plan to make parallel tests on other sets of ratings, *viz.,* those derived from a "holistic" interpretation of the need-interviews, from an analysis of the case histories, from an analysis of the TAT protocols, and from conference judgments based upon all three sources of information.

Furthermore, each of the 388 correlations noted in Table 4 represents a specific subhypothesis. Before reporting on these subhypotheses, we wish to note the kind and degree of correlation between the specific subvariables at the different levels of personality tapped by the three kinds of information. Let us illustrate the nature of this line of further investigation. From the ratings of Ktsanes and Ktsanes we have found significantly positive correlations between husband's overt succorance and wife's overt nurturance, but the reverse correlations (husband's overt nurturance with wife's overt succorance) were nonsignificant. It is of considerable interest to determine whether or not this pattern obtains at considerably deeper levels of personality.

In our research design we have also provided for a descriptive phase of the study. The major purposes of this phase are to illuminate the processes underlying the verified hypotheses and to provide material for the generating of new and more refined hypotheses. The descriptive phase consists of (*a*) the most complete and intensive analysis of each subject's personality which our materials and talents will permit and (*b*) a case-by-case analysis of the degree of "meshing" of the personalities of the spouses.

TABLE 1: *Summary of 344 Interspousal Correlations Involving Pairs of Needs or Traits*
(For all r's, H: r>0)*

	Number of Permutations		Total in Hypothesized Direction	Number of r's			
				Significant in:			
				Hypothesized Direction		Opposite Direction	
Paried Variables	Total	Tested		.01	.05	.01	.05
Two Needs							
Abasement-Autonomy	32	24	23	—	3	—	—
Abasement-Dominance	32	16	14	7	12	—	—
Abasement-Hostility	32	24	22	3	8	2	5
Abasement-Nurturance	32	24	5	—	—	—	—
Abasement-Recognition	32	16	7	1	2	—	—
Achievement-Deference	16	8	6	—	—	—	2
Achievement-Dominance	16	8	2	—	1	—	—
Achievement-Recognition	16	8	4	—	1	—	—
Achievement-Status Aspiration	4	4	—	—	—	—	—
Autonomy-Deference	32	24	19	—	2	—	—
Autonomy-Hostility	32	16	9	—	1	—	—
Deference-Dominance	32	32	32	12	20	—	—
Deference-Hostility	32	8	7	2	3	—	—
Deference-Nurturance	32	24	5	—	—	1	5
Deference-Recognition	32	24	9	1	2	—	—

Dominance-Succorance	32	24	17	—	1	2	—	—
Nurturance-Succorance	32	24	20	—	—	2	—	—
Status Aspiration-Status Striving	2	2	—	—	—	—	—	—
Two Traits								
Anxiety-Emotionality	8	8	2	—	1	—	—	
One Need and One Trait								
Achievement-Vicariousness	8	4	4	—	—	—	—	
Dominance-Vicariousness	16	4	4	1	2	—	—	
Nurturance-Anxiety	16	12	6	—	1	—	—	
Recognition-Vicariousness	16	4	2	—	—	—	—	
Status Striving-Vicariousness	4	2	2	—	1	—	—	
Total	538	344	221	28	63	3	12	

*Since a double-dichotomized variable consists of four subvariables, there are 32 possible interspousal correlations. For example, each of the four abasement scores on husbands may be correlated with each of the four autonomy scores on wives. This gives 16 interspousal correlations. The other 16 correlations result from pairing each of the four abasement scores on wives with each of the four autonomy scores on husbands.

The number of correlations reported in the column headed "Total in Hypothesized Direction" involves all r's of the appropriate sign, irrespective of whether or not they are adjudged to be significant.

Since a one-sided hypothesis is being tested, r's are reported in the "Hypothesized Direction" column when they are of the proper sign and equal or exceed the critical values: $r_{.01} = .46$ and $r_{.05} = .34$ (df = 23).

Experimentally the r's reported in the "Opposite Direction" columns constitute negative evidence. A two-sided test was used to determine their significance with $r_{.01} = .51$ and $r_{.05} = .40$. For this reason the frequencies in the "hypothesized" and "opposite" directions columns are not comparable.

Thus row 1 of the table may be read as follows. There are 32 possible interspousal correlations involving the variables abasement and autonomy. Of these 32, positive signs were hypothesized for 24 and these 24 correlations were computed. Twenty-three of the 24 coefficients were positive. Three of them exceeded .34, and none was greater than .46. None of the 24 was in the negative direction than .40 (and indeed only one was negative).

TABLE 2: *Summary of Interspousal Correlations Involving the Correlation of a Need or Trait with Itself*
(For all r's, H: r<0)*

Variable	Number of Permutations Total	Tested	Total in Hypothesized Direction	Number of r's — Significant in: Hypothesized Direction .01	.05	Opposite Direction .01	.05
Needs							
Abasement	16	4	4	2	3	—	—
Achievement	4	2	2	—	—	—	—
Approach	4	2	—	—	—	1	1
Autonomy	16	4	2	2	—	—	—
Deference	16	4	3	—	2	—	—
Dominance	16	4	4	—	—	—	1
Hostility	16	4	3	—	—	—	—
Nuturance	16	4	3	—	—	—	—
Recognition	16	4	4	2	2	—	—
Succorance	16	4	4	—	—	—	1
Status Aspiration	1	1	—	—	—	—	—
Status Striving	1	1	1	—	—	—	—

Traits

Anxiety	4	2	1	—	—	1	1
Emotionality	4	2	2	—	1	—	—
Vicariousness	4	2	2	—	—	—	2
Total	150	44	35	6	8	2	4

TABLE 3: *Summary of 388 Interspousal Correlations (From Tables 1 and 2)*[1]

	Number of Permutations		Total in Hypothesized Direction	Number of r's Significant in:			
				Hypothesized Direction		Opposite Direction	
Kind of Interpousal Correlation	Total	Tested		.01	.05	.01	.05
Two Needs or Traits[2]	538	344	221	28	63	3	12
One Need or Trait[3]	150	44	35	6	8	2	4
Total	688	388	256	34	71	5	16

[1] For explanations of columns, see footnote to Table 1.
[2] From Table 1. It was hypothesized that these correlations would be positive.
[3] From Table 2. It was hypothesized that these correlations would be negative.

TABLE 4: *Observed and Expected Distributions of Hypothesized Coefficients of Correlation at .01 and .05 Levels*[1]

Coefficients of Correlation	.01 Level		.05 Level	
	Observed	Expected	Observed	Expected
Significant in hypothesized direction	34	3.88	71	19.40
Other	354	384.12	317	368.60
Total	388	388.00	388	388.00
Chi-square[2]	$228.40 \sim p < .001$		$141.68 \sim p < .001$	

[1]Because the sign is hypothesized, a one-tailed significance test is used. N = 25; df = 23; $r._{01} = .46$; $r._{05} = .34$. The chi-square value for the .01 level is probably too high because the value of the expected frequency in the upper cell is less than the usually stated minimum of 5. If the value of 5 were substituted for 3.88, however, the chi-square would still have a value corresponding to p < .001. It may be argued, moreover, that since these correlations are all based on 25 couples or 50 persons, it is incorrect to apply the test which involves the assumption that the coefficients are independent. It is true that

the variance of the corresponding z's exceeds the theoretical value of $\dfrac{1}{n-3}$ as might be expected in a case of nonindependence. When the empirical $s^2.z$

(= .09397) is substituted for the theoretical, however, the number of significant correlations still exceeds the chance expectation. For example, 12 are significant at the .01 level, yielding a significant chi-square of 15.116. This chi-square would still be significant at the .01 level if we raised the theoretical value in the upper cell from 3.88 to 5.

[2]Yates' correction for discontinuity has been applied.

NOTES

1. This implication has been stated as follows: "people desire children for reasons largely unknown to themselves and . . . these reasons, if they can be uncovered, will be of considerable value in illuminating the ways in which parents act toward their children and react to them, the ways in which they participate in the formation of the personality structures of their children." R. F. Winch, "The Study of Personality in the Family Setting," *Social Forces,* 28 (1950), p. 314.

2. H. A. Murray et al., *Explorations in Personality,* New York: Oxford University Press, 1938.

3. The theory of complementary needs may be extended beyond mate-selection and the dyad. It would appear feasible to make use of the general form of the theory in explaining the formation of cliques within groups, in selecting working teams as for bomber crews, and the like.

4. In our formulation "sex" is not the equivalent of "love," and hence the latter is not a euphemism for the former. Sexual needs are certainly important, but we do not conceive of them as constituting the totality of "important psychic needs." The importance of sex, relative to other needs, varies from marriage to marriage and from person to person, and within persons its relative importance varies from moment to moment and from level to level of consciousness.

5. "Field of eligibles" is explained below.

6. Nurturant means giving sympathy, help, protection, or indulgence, and succorant means seeking the same things.

7. Complementary needs as a basis of mate-selection have occasionally been remarked among neurotic spouses, wherein we might speak of the "theory of complementary neuroses." (*Cf., eg.,* C. P. Oberndorf, "Psychoanalysis of Married Couples," *Psychoanalytic Review,* 25 (1938), pp. 453–57). It is our hypothesis, however, that complementariness operates among so-called normals as well as among neurotics.

8. Murray, Explorations p. 124.

9. Definitions of the needs and general traits used in this study appear in both of the previous publications on the theory of complementary needs. (*Cf.* R. F. Winch, *The Modern Family,* New York: Holt, 1952, Ch. 15; T. Ktsanes and V. Ktsanes, "The Theory of Complementary Needs in Mate-Selection," in R. F. Winch and R. McGinnis (eds.), *Selected Studies in Marriage and the Family,* New York: Holt, 1953, pp. 435–53.) The needs used in the quantitative analysis presented below are abasement, achievement, approach, autonomy, deference, dominance, hostility, nurturance, recognition, status aspiration, status striving, and succorance; the general traits are anxiety, emotionality, and vicariousness. Although we conceive of sex as a need, we have not treated it quantitatively in the present study. The reason for this is that in the clinical literature and in our impressionistic preconceptions the sex drive seems to assume myriad forms, and hence to conceptualize it as a unidimensional continuum seems to do unusual violence to the phenomenon under study.

10. Ktsanes and Ktsanes, "Complimentary Needs," p. 442. At first reading it might appear that high need recognition equals low need deference, and hence that case 1 is similar to case 2. We do not, however, regard

recognition and deference as poles of the same dimension; rather, it seems quite possible for a person to be high on both or low on both of these variables.

11. For interpretive summaries of these studies see: Winch, *The Modern Family*, pp. 400–403; and Ktsanes and Ktsanes, "Complementary Needs," pp. 435–438. A more extensive bibliography on assortative mating appears in A. B. Hollingshead, "Cultural Factors in the Selection of Marriage Mates," *American Sociological Review*, 15 (1950), 619–20. Although there is abundant evidence to support the hypothesis of homogamy with respect to such social characteristics as those noted above, the studies which have concerned emotional and motivational characteristics of mate-selection have not yielded conclusive evidence for either homogamy or heterogamy.

12. It will be noted that "need" as used in this context is not synonymous with "interest." It seems plausible that mate-selection tends to pair people with similar interests (as for bridge, classical music, fundamentalist religion, and the like). In other words, (*a*) we accept the evidence which points to intramarital *homo*geneity with respect to social characteristics, (*b*) we think it plausible that there is also intra-marital *homo*geneity with respect to interests, but (*c*) we hypothesize that there is intramarital *hetero*geneity with respect to such motivational dimensions as those cited in n. 9 above. It seems plausible to suspect that, other things being equal, persons who are homogeneous with respect to social characteristics and interests would be more likely to gratify each other's needs than would persons who are heterogeneous in such respects. For a more complete exposition of the theory of complementary needs see Winch, *The Modern Family*. Ch. 12 and esp. Ch. 15; and Ktsanes and Ktsanes, "Complementary Needs." An illustrative case appears in each of these references.

13. The degree of inter-rater reliability is indicated by the fact that the median of the 44 uncorrected correlations between the two raters was .60; the range was from .33 to .84.

14. Schools such as music and education were excluded from the defined population because of our suspicion that they might exercise an atypical selective bias. In 1950 there was a considerable number of married undergraduate students, most of whom were veterans.

15. The population consists of (*a*) married undergraduate students in selected schools of Northwestern University with certain specified social characteristics and (*b*) the spouses of these students irrespective of the latter's social characteristics. The specified characteristics are: white race, middle class background (as revealed by father's occupation), within 19–26 age range, second or later generation native-born, and Christian or no specified religion.

16. Although we feel perfectly justified in this application of the one-tailed test of significance, questions concerning its application have arisen in the literature (*Cf.*, *e.g.*, C. J. Burke, "A Brief Note on One-Tailed Tests," *Psychological Bulletin*, 50 (1953), pp. 384–87, and the references cited there.) Since there may be readers who are skeptical concerning the applicability of the one-tailed test in this situation, we show the data below set up for the two-tailed test and note that the results are just as conclusive.

Coefficients of Correlation	.01 Level		.05 Level	
	Observed	Expected	Observed	Expected
In hypothesized direction				
Significant	28	1.94	53	9.70
Nonsignificant	228	192.06	203	184.30
In opposite direction				
Nonsignificant	127	192.06	116	184.30
Significant	5	1.94	16	9.70
Total	388	388.00	388	388.00
Chi-square	383.66 ~ p <.001		224.59 ~ p <.001	

Critical values for two-tailed test : $r_{.01} = .51$; $r_{.05} = .40$. In the top and bottom cells of the .01 column the expected frequencies are below the desired minimum. If these values are raised from 1.94 to 5, the resulting chi-square still greatly exceeds that needed for significance at the .001 level.

2 Psychological Patterning in Marriage

ROLAND G. THARP

After seventy years of research, the broad outlines of a systematic social science approach to marriage may be discerned. Both psychology and sociology have made extensive explorations. Before us now is the task of integration, which should map the work of both disciplines into appropriate relations with one another. Like early cartographers, we shall err; but a solid ground of data exists, and can be distinguished from unknown seas.

Marriage research began in the 1890s with Pearson's comparisons of the anthropometric characteristics of spouses. From that time until our own, the organizing issue in all mating research has remained the same, namely, the degree of similarity between husband and wives. That is, do "likes marry likes" (homogamy), or do "unlikes" marry (heterogamy)?

From *Psychological Bulletin,* Vol. 60, No. 2, March 1963, pp. 97–117. Copyright 1963 by the American Psychological Association.

Sociology has produced convincing evidence for homogamy of several cultural variables. Hollingshead (1950) has provided both an excellent bibliography and a definitive piece of research demonstrating homogamy with respect to race, age, religion, ethnic origin, and social class. More recently, residential propinquity has been added to sociological variables influencing mate selection; Katz and Hill (1958) provide a bibliography, a review, and an integration. These factors, then, largely define that pool of opposite-sex individuals which one is most likely to meet and know; it may be called the "field of eligibles" (Winch, 1952).

Yet it is obvious that the individual psychology must be accountable to some degree for the "field of acquaintances" from which the mate must ultimately be selected. Psychological factors must affect the limits of the field, and most certainly selection from within those limits. It is perhaps such considerations that have led sociologists to extend their investigations to *psychological* factors affecting mate selection and marriage outcome.

Such investigations began in the 1920s. The pioneering work of Burgess and Cottrell, King, Locke, Terman, Kirkpatrick, and others has been presented and summarized in Burgess and Wallin's important book, *Engagement and Marriage* (1953), which also reports the results of their own study of 1,000 engaged and 666 married couples.

In all these early studies, homogamy—not heterogamy—is the trend, though relationships are of a low order among psychological variables—much lower than for the investigated cultural characteristics and social traits. For example, Burgess and Wallin reported that of the 42 items of the Thurstone Neurotic Inventory, 14 showed a greater than chance expectation for homogamy of engaged couples. None were heterogamous. The significant relationships ranged (in ratio of obtained to expected similarity) from 1.17 on "do you day-dream frequently?" to 1.04 on "when you were in school did you hesitate to volunteer in a class recitation?" Comparable results are reported for items on the Bernreuter Personality Inventory and the Strong Interest Test by Terman (1938). Homogamy, then, obtains in *assortative mating*.

Marital success was at that time (and remains) the second outcome variable of interest to researchers. Generalizing from the studies of Terman (1938), Terman and Oden (1947), and Burgess and Wallin (1953, p. 529), the latter authors present the following lists of characteristics as the most decisive in differentiating happy from unhappy marriages:

Happily Married	Unhappily Married
Emotionally stable	Emotionally unstable
Considerate of others	Critical of others
Yielding	Dominating
Companionable	Isolated
Self-confident	Lacking self-confidence
Emotionally dependent	Emotionally self-sufficient

Employing the Thurstone items (obtained before marriage) weighted for maximum discrimination, Burgess and Wallin report correlations with marital success scores of .25 for men and .18 for women. Bernreuter responses, after marriage, provide success correlations of .38 and .42 for the sexes, respectively, according to Terman. The Burgess and Wallin results were substantially replicated more than 20 years later on a grossly different sample by Burchinal, Hawkes, and Gardner (1957). That individuals' neurotic traits are predictive of marital disharmony can be accepted as a demonstrated fact.

The generalization "homogamy-with-respect-to-personality-traits" is drawn by all the classic investigators. It should be remembered, however, that most traits investigated are neurotic in character. That neurotics unite in marriage with neurotics is an observation common in psychoanalytic literature. In the light of our present knowledge of the relationships between culture and personality, homogamy of the degree reported with respect to social interests and general personality traits could likely be accounted for on the basis of the common modal personalities of individuals in common cultural groups; particularly when it is known that these cultural similarities establish the marital field of eligibles. The effect of degrees of homogamy or heterogamy on marital success has not been assessed, beyond the fact that individuals possessing those traits listed in the right-hand column above are more likely to be unhappily married, and are likely to be married homogamously, and are thereby doubly damned.

The main body of this review, then, is concerned with studies having the the above-summarized information as background. More recent research can conveniently be divided into four somewhat overlapping areas: interpersonal perception, identification, complementary needs, and role theory.

INTERPERSONAL PERCEPTION

Perception of the self and of others has lately been a central construct in influential theories and research of personality and personality change (Rogers and Dymond, 1954). Although the classic studies discussed above have used self-ratings and ratings-by-others as techniques in marriage research, Kelly (1941) was the first to consider perception of personality as an operative force in its own right: "the actual relative position of the husband and wife on a personality trait continuum are not as important in determining compatibility as the belief of the husband and wife regarding their relative positions on these scales" (p. 193). The instrument used to investigate this proposition was Kelly's 36-item Personality Rating Scale, administered for self-perception and perception of spouse to 76 couples. His results may be summarized as follows: subjects rate themselves less favorably than they rate their spouses, and less favorably than they are rated *by* their spouses. The Burgess-Terman-Miles Compatibility Index was also administered to

each subject, yielding the following information: high compatibility is associated with more favorable self-ratings, but accompanied by spouse ratings which are yet more favorable. These
findings hold true for both husband and wife. Kelly concludes
that an individual's personal satisfaction in marriage is related
both to self-regard and to the judgment of the self's inferiority
or superiority vis-à-vis the spouse.

Preston, Peltz, Mudd, and Froscher (1952) extended this
type of investigation to the consideration of the relationship
between person-perception and objective appraisal of that person. Couples drawn from the clients of the Marriage Council of
Philadelphia constituted the sample. Fifty-five couples had received premarital counseling; 116 had received postmarital
counseling. The two groups can be accepted as more-and less-
happily married subjects. Using a personality rating scale of 17
items—selected from those used by Kelly (1941), and Burgess
and Cottrell (1939)—Kelly's results were substantially
verified, except that the less-happily married man judged their
wives much more severely than themselves. This discrepancy
seems in principle to conform with Kelly's formulation. The
difference in range of happiness to be expected between the
samples of the two studies would seem to account for this
disparate finding.

Further results are as follows:

1. Self-ratings of spouses show positive correlations of the
same order as those of the classic studies with a tendency for
greater congruence in happier than in unhappy couples.
(Medians=.19 and .30, respectively.)

2. Higher correlations occur, however, between ratings-of-
self and ratings-of-spouse. This tendency is likewise stronger
with more happily-marrieds.

Concerning the question of objectivity of perception, Preston
et al. (1952) comment as follows:

The correlations between the self-ratings of the spouses are
uniformly much less than the correlations between the ratings of
self and partner no matter which spouse is studied. Further, the

data of the experiment indicate conclusively that the happily
married group exhibit a larger discrepancy between the relevant
correlation coefficients. From these two facts the conclusion is
inescapable that the happily married groups show more evidence
of lack of realism in their personality appraisals than the unhappily married group (p. 335).

This conclusion becomes quite inescapable when one realizes
that the self as seen by the self, and the self as seen by the
spouse, necessarily constitute different stimulus patterns; there
is no reason to expect total agreement. Further, it is somewhat
risky to invoke "realism" as a consideration when none of the
variables concerned are externally validated. Rather, these
data indicate a perceived similarity of self and spouse *as they
interact,* such similarity increasing with marital happiness.

Dymond's (1954) data seem to support this view. She concludes: "Married love is not blind . . . the better each partner
understands the other's perceptions of himself and his world,
the more satisfactory the relationship" (p. 171). Her subjects
were 15 couples well known to her, with a mean length of
marriage of 10.4 years. One hundred MMPI items, pertaining
to interaction with others, were administered to each of the 30
subjects. After answering for the self, each subject predicted
the spouse's answers. In order to control for stereotype of
reply, all items which were answered uniformly by more than
two-thirds of the group were eliminated, leaving 55 items
exhibiting a reasonable degree of difference. Since the yes-or-
no probabilities of these items were roughly equal, predictive
ability ("understanding") would be uncontaminated by knowledge of group norms. Scores were then related to the happiness
of the marriage, as rated by the subjects themselves and validated by Dymond's rating. The usual finding occurred: happily married spouses resembled each other more than unhappily
marrieds. Dymond's principal hypothesis was verified also;
happys predict spouse replies significantly better than do un-
happys. Further, there is significantly less association between
similarity of self-spouse and accuracy of prediction in the
happy than in the unhappy group.

It can be seen from the foregoing studies that with increases in self-similarity, increases of perceived self-similarity and increases in predictive ability, happiness is greater. But all research indicates that, presumably due to patterns of assortative mating, the two selves of the partners—happy or no—exhibit similarity. The inference seems, therefore, that happiness increases as does congruence between self-as-self and self-as-spouse. Put differently, when the self as seen by the self and the self as seen by the spouse become more nearly equal stimulus configurations; that is, when the self, acting as spouse, does no violence to self-identity, then, either causatively or concomitantly, happiness increases. Considerations such as these will be expounded more fully under the section on role theory below.

Corsini's (1956a, 1956b) important and startling results allow further generalizations. Twenty volunteer students and their spouses, from the University of Chicago, participated. Marital happiness was assessed by the Burgess-Wallin scale. A 50-item adjective Q sort was sorted four times by each subject: (*a*) for self, (*b*) for spouse, (*c*) prediction for spouse, and— adding a new dimension to previous research—(*d*) prediction of the spouse's description of the subject. A long-overdue experimental control was instituted by Corsini: every conclusion with repect to couples was checked by drawing random samples of noncouples, and the same operations for couples duplicated. Following previous investigators, Corsini agrees that: (*a*) understanding the mate is not related to similarity of self and mate, and (*b*) happiness is associated with similarity of self-perceptions.

However, Corsini (1956a, 1956b) discovered that although understanding can be shown to exist between husbands and wives, this understanding is related to marital happiness only in those comparisons when the *husband* is the target of Q sorts (that is, wife's prediction $\times$ husband's self-perception; and husband's prediction $\times$ wife's perception of him). In these instances, husband-wife correlations vary positively with marital happiness for both mates. This strongly suggests that the husband's role in marriage is the crucial one for the satisfaction of both partners. However, the above-stated relationship was then shown by Corsini to be no more true for husband and wife than for randomly-paired men and women who did not even know each other! This led him to suggest that the relevant relationship may exist between marital happiness and a *stereotyped* conception of the husband. He then demonstrated that the greater "conformity" of male self-perception (measured by the mean correlation for each male against all other males) is positively correlated with happiness for both husband and wife. None of these relationships hold when perceptions of the female is the variable considered.

It seems, therefore, that our prior generalization can be expanded. The congruence, necessary for happiness, between self-perception and perception by the spouse is particularly crucial for the male; further, this agreement as to male-as-husband most often partakes liberally of widely-shared expectations of husbandly qualities.

Luckey (1959, 1960a, 1960b), in her careful and impressive study, contributes to this emerging formulation. Eighty-one couples, all of some education at the University of Minnesota, were selected from a much larger subject-pool in order to provide two groups highly differentiated on the Locke and Terman marital happiness scales. The Leary Interpersonal Check List (ICL) was completed by each subject for self, spouse, ideal self, mother, and father. Congruence or divergence between a respondent and these "significant others" could be estimated on each of four scales provided by the ICL. Luckey's results support Corsini's. Satisfaction in marriage is related to the congruence of the husband's self-concept and that held of him by the wife. The relation does not hold for concepts of wives. Happiness is also related to (*a*) congruence of the husband's self and ideal concepts, (*b*) congruence of husband's self-concept and his concept of his father, and (*c*) congruence of the wives' concepts of their husbands and concepts of their fathers.

It seems, therefore, that the maximally happy marital situation can be described as follows: husband and wife agree that he is as *he* wishes to be, namely, like his father; and as *she* wishes him to be, namely, like her's. Surely this broad area of agreement is the culturally defined male sex-role—more specifically, the male subrole of husband.

IDENTIFICATION

The mechanism whereby appropriate sex-typical behaviors are transmitted from one generation to another has long been labeled "identification." The psychoanalytic account of the process involved is the most elaborate: the boy renounces a direct libidinal claim upon the mother in favor of vicarious gratification through the father, with whom he thus "identifies"; thereby establishing congruent values and behaviors between boy and specific father, and also between the boy and the general male gender. The process for the girl is held to be similar, though more gradual, and culminating not in a preschool climax, but in a diffused struggling until late adolescence or early marriage, when the female identity crisis must be met.

In any case, the child renounces strong libidinal cathexes upon the opposite-sex parent. The obvious inference for mate selection has been repeatedly drawn: the courtship quest is for the opposite-sex parent image (Dreikurs, 1930; Fluegel, 1926; Hamilton and McGowan, 1930). Sporadic and generally unsuccessful efforts to test this hypothesis have been made. Hamilton and McGowan (1930) reproted that only 17% of men studied did marry women bearing physical resemblances to their mothers. Of these men, however, 94% were happy, whereas only 33% of the men were happy when mates did not resemble mothers. A similar, though only slight, relationship held between happiness and wife's similarity to mother's temperament.

If men marry mother's images, would not sons of younger mothers marry younger women than sons of older mothers? Commins (1932), using 1,075 subjects of the English *Who's Who,* reported statistically significant younger age at marriage for oldest sons as compared to other-than-oldest sons. Kirkpatrick (1937), using 768 cases from the *Compendium of Amer-*

ican Genealogy, found no relationship between sibling position and mean age at marriage. Mangus (1936), using 600 college women as subjects, found that, on matters of interests and personality traits, women rate their ideal-as-husband more similarly to their current most intimate male companion than to their fathers. We may conclude, with Sears (1942), that there are as yet no statistical investigations which are adequate for purposes of verifying the mate–opposite sex parent resemblances notion.

The more recent investigation by Strauss (1946a, 1946b), though, did give new life to the issue. A group of 373 engaged, informally engaged, or recently married persons (200 women, 173 men) participated. Strauss reports greater resemblances between men's mothers and mates than between women's fathers and mates, but this information was garnered by simply asking the subjects how much resemblance existed—"very much" to "not at all." Responses less subject to bias, fortunately, were obtained on 25 personality traits, rated by each subject separately for self, mate, and parents. These data give evidence for something more than chance congruence between personalities of mate and parent, *but not necessarily of the opposite sex parent.* On the basis of interviews conducted with some female subjects, Strauss suggests that childhood affectional experiences with parents are linked with adult love choices.

The precise nature of this link seems to be the processes of identification. The Burgess-Wallin (1953) data, studied by Lu (1952c), indicate that parental authority–domination, as reported by the offspring, is positively related to childhood conflict with the parent, and negatively related to adult attachment to that parent, irrespective of the sex of parent or child. These conclusions were based on the several items in the Burgess-Wallin questionnaire which bore face validity to the dimensions investigated. This limitation, plus the evident opportunity for the subjects to respond with halo, would lead a reader to withhold judgment on Lu's hypotheses. However, precisely this relationship is being demonstrated in current developmental-longitudinal studies of identification processes (Kagan, 1958;

Payne and Mussen, 1956). Apparently it is affectional bonds which leads the boy to identify with the father, not fear of his castrating ire.

Earlier, we proposed that identification with the father leads to happier marriage. Assuming that early affectional relationships with the father lead to stronger identification, we would expect that such an affectional relationship would affect marital happiness.

Luckey's results are pertinent here (Luckey, 1960a, 1960b). In the unhappy marriages which she studied, men saw their fathers as more dominant and less loving than themselves on each of the ICL scales. Lu's further work suggests one of the consequences of conflict with parents (Lu, 1952b). By the use of a 16-item dominance-submission scale, he divided marriages into husband-dominant, equalitarian, and wife-dominant groups. Dominant roles are associated with conflict with parents, equalitarian roles associated with affectional attachment to parents. Further, there is good evidence for equalitarian roles' positive association with marital adjustment, and dominant roles', by either spouse, negative association with marital adjustment (Lu, 1952a).

Obviously, so few studies have been done in this area that only the most tentative general hypotheses can be extracted. But it does not seem untoward to propose the following. Solid affectional father–son bonds lead to the adoption, by the youth, of the ways of the male. This allows him, as husband, to be thoroughly himself while enacting the expected male role as husband. This satisfactory performance of husband role satisfies the expectations of the wife; the husband too is happy, for the self–as–self and the self–as–spouse produce no conflict. Under such circumstances, no submissive or compensating-dominating patterns of relationship need be instituted. The possible permutations of the few variables used here lead to a myriad of predictions, none of which could be checked by data now available. (Though it should be mentioned that a pattern of early affectional relationships leading to a predominantly cross-sexual identification—at least in the male—would be expected to lead to results opposite to those outlined above.)

COMPLEMENTARY NEEDS

A new and vigorous dissident entered the homogamy–heterogamy issue in the person of R. F. Winch, who with his associates has elaborated the theory of complementary needs. Briefly stated, the theory holds that though homogamy of social characteristics establishes a "field of eligibles," mate selection within this field is determined by a specific kind of *heterogamy of motives*—complementarity. This complementarity may be of two kinds: (*a*) that in which partners differ in *degree* of the same need, or (*b*) differ in *kind* of need. That mate is selected who offers the greatest probability of providing maximum need satisfaction, as the partners act according to their complementary pattern of motives: "So that if individuals A and B have complementary need patterns, B's resulting behavior will be a greater source of gratification to A than will be the case with the behavior of C, who is psychically similar to A" (Winch, Ktsanes, and Ktsanes, 1954, p. 242).

In marriage research, no other hypothesis produced in the last decade has been as influential: "(Winch's) work represents a valuable entree to an extremely complex and subtle problem area . . . not only to family studies, but to many other problem areas as well, notably personality types and the division of labor, cohesion in small groups, stable marginal adjustments, etc." (Rosow, 1957, p. 232). "It is through this fulfillment-of-complementary-needs approach that further sociological studies should bear fruit" (Kephart, 1957). Application of the CN approach is being made to the field of marital counseling and social work (Meyer, 1957; Winch, M., 1958). The Winch group has amassed some 11 separate publications treating complementarity; several dissertations; engendered four critical articles; and numerous derivative studies, at least four of which have been published.

Yet no thorough appraisal of the data on which the theory of CN is based has appeared.[1] That will be the next task of this review. Now let us examine Winch's procedures.

The sample is described as: "Twenty-five married undergraduate students in selected schools of Northwestern University of white race, middle class background, 19–26 years of age, second or later generation native-born of Christian or no specified religion; and their spouses" (Winch, Ktsanes, and Ktsanes, 1954). Twelve "needs" from Murray's well-known list, as well as three "general traits" were studied. Most of these variables were "double-dichotomized," that is, rated separately for being operative *within* or *without* the marriage, and separately for operating *overtly* or *covertly*, yielding 44 subvariables.

Three techniques were employed to garner information from which the 44 subvariables could be quantified. First came the need interview, a structured interview from which the following are the published sample questions: "how do you feel when someone steps in front of you in queue in a crowded restaurant"; and "how do you feel when you see your name in print" (Winch, 1958).

Second, a case-history interview was conducted. This (Winch, 1958), "began with the subject's earliest memories, covered his perceptions and experiences with key familial and other figures, and brought him through his various developmental stages to the present moment" (p. 110).

Thirdly, eight TAT cards were administered. (It should be noted that the Cattell 16 PF, Form A, was also included, but of this we hear only a 1958 footnote characterizing the results as "largely negative" (Winch, 1958, p. 110).

Each subject was given a separate rating on each variable for the need interview (NI-1); for the case history (CH), and for the TAT (TAT-O). The quantifying techniques for each should be noted. For NI-1, two judges rated each subvariable on a 1–5 scale. Interjudge reliability is reported as .60. Ratings were summed and normalized (Winch, Ktsanes, and Ktsanes, 1954).

For the TAT, the same procedure—content analysis—was followed. Interrater reliabilities were reported as in the range of .20 (Winch and More, 1956a, 1956b). "This procedure was undertaken with essentially negative results" (Winch, 1958, p. 110). Following this (Winch, 1958) we undertook a mode of analysis on the need-interview, the case-history interview, and the TAT which might be called "global" or "molar" or "clinical" or "projective" or "holistic." A different analyst worked on each of these three sources of information and sought, as far as the data would allow, to create a complete dynamic analysis of each subject . . . after writing such a report and on the basis of the analysis he had prepared, each analyst would then rate the subject on the 44 sub-variables (pp. 110–111);

thus, NI-2; CH; and TAT-C.

Still another set of ratings was to come—the FC (full-case conference).

In order to arrive at a psychodynamic interpretation and a set of ratings for each subject in which we could place our greatest confidence, we formed a clinical conference of five persons . . . each analyst read and criticized all three written reports . . . inconsistencies were discussed, and relevant evidence was examined . . . after arriving at what might be called "diagnostic" consensus, all five analysts agreed on a final set of ratings of the subjects' needs (Winch, 1958, p. 111).

Thus, six sets of ratings are available. Five are subsequently reported.[2]

The FC was used as the criterion for validity of the other indices. The general range of correlations between FC ratings and other sets are as follows: NI-1, .60; NI-2, .80; CH, .74; and TAC-C, .00 (Winch and More, 1956).

The hypotheses to be tested with these data were derived from the theory of CN. The statistical technique was the interspousal product–moment correlation, i.e., husband's subvariable scores times their respective wives subvariable scores. Of 1,936 possible interspousal correlations, 388 were hypothesized as to direction of sign: 344, involving *different* needs or traits, would be *positive* in sign; 44 involving the *same* need or trait, would be *negative* (Winch, Ktsanes, and Ktsanes, 1954). The specific relationships hypothesized have not been published. The general validity of the CN theory was staked on a chi square test for greater-than-chance occurrence of signs of correlations in the hypothesized directions.

The results of interspousal correlational distributions NI-1, NI-2, and FC met this chi square test. CH did not. For TAT-C, the directionality of the distribution was reversed. Winch (1955a) concludes that "the bulk of the evidence, therefore, supports the hypothesis that mates tend to select each other on the basis of complementary needs" (p. 554).

A further analysis followed. Constructing a Q-type matrix, the correlations for variables could be compared for married pairs versus nonmarried pairs. In this matrix of 625 male–female correlations, 25 were of the former, 600 of the latter group. Testing for same-variable correlations, CN theory would predict lower (and presumably negative) correlations for marrieds, and higher for nonmarried. In addition to comparing the 25 to the 600, Winch also randomly matched each man with a woman not his wife and compared these correlations with the 25 husband–wife coefficients. In both cases, the NI-1 data demonstrate statistically significant difference between mates' and nonmates' mean correlations and in the hypothesized directions. The FC data do not show such differences. The NI-1 results are as follows: mean husband–wife correlation, .1016; mean man–woman correlation, .2316. The range of the husband–wife coefficients is from + .52 to − .32. Nine of these were negative, 16 positive.

Cluster analyses (Winch, Ktsanes, and Ktsanes, 1955), R-type factor analysis (Roos, 1957), and Q-type factor analysis (Ktsanes, 1955) have been performed on the Winch data. All results have been summarized in *Mate Selection: A Study of Complementary Needs* (Winch, 1958). This volume also contains speculative elaboration of CN theory, detailed case reports, etc.

Now certain exceptions must be taken when it is maintained that the case for complementary needs theory has been demonstrated:

1. Sample—Of what population can 25 married undergraduate couples be taken as representative?

2. Ratings—"(Of the correlations) an indeterminate num-

ber could actually have been spurious reflections of the raters' implicit theories of trait organization" (Katz, Glucksberg, and Krauss, 1960, p. 205). This appraisal by Katz et al. was earlier voiced by Strodtbeck (1959). Bowman (1955) and Kernodle (1959) have complained that sociologists, by the nature of their training, are not qualified to undertake psychological analyses such as an investigation of complementary needs requires. Perhaps; but researches are to be judged by their fruit rather than their roots. Yet this psychologist cannot but wish that more account had been taken of the problems of rater subjectivity—bias, projection, halo; as well as the issues of reliability and validity: in short, all the concerns of those who deal in objective psychological assessment.

3. Statistics—Aside from the probable nonindependent nature of the variables, built in by the rating technique, there is the question of statistical nonindependence. In a distribution of intercorrelations, when Variables A and B are positively related, and likewise B and C, the relation between A and C cannot be taken as an independent event. In a matrix of 1,936 correlations which are positively related throughout (Winch & More, 1956a, 1956b), the 388 "tests" were not selected on a basis of posited independence of event, but without regard to this issue. Winch (1958) has recognized this problem, but commented that, "Just how many independent events there are is a very complex question" (p. 115). We agree.

4. Results—The data, taken as they have been rated, analyzed, and reported do not support the CN hypothesis. Winch concludes that he is upheld by the bulk of the evidence—NI-1, NI-2, and FC; and not supported by only CH and TAT-C. Are not, however, NI-1 and NI-2 in reality two ratings on only one datum? And are they not correlated an average of .60 and .80 with the third supporting set, FC? Rather than winning by 3 to 2, complementarity appears to have lost by 3 to 1. (And if one is to consider TAT-O and the 16 PF results, the score becomes even more embarrassing.)

5. Research Philosophy—Almost any set of data, if sufficiently badgered, can be exhausted into submission.

6. Other Research—Bowerman and Day (1956), using 60

couples who were either formally engaged or regular dating partners and who were drawn as volunteers from college sociology classes, attempted to test the CN hypothesis. Their instrument was the Edwards Personal Preference Schedule (EPPS); this offered an objective measurement of 10 of the needs used by Winch, as both Edwards and Winch drew from Murray's need list. On same-need matching, more evidence for homogamy than for complementarity was found; on different-need matchings, no evidence for either principle of organization was unearthed.

Winch (1957) insisted that this constitutes no replication, on the following grounds: (*a*) The EPPS, "though ingeniously conceived—has no known validity for measuring needs." Two other objections smack less of the pot and the kettle: (*b*) the Bowerman and Day subjects were not yet married; and (*c*) the variables used were not identical (p. 336).

The objections have been answered by Schellenberg and Bee (1960). One hundred college couples were investigated. Sixty-four were recently married, 18 engaged, and 18 were going steady. The EPPS was again the measuring device. Considering the marrieds and unmarrieds separately, and the 100 couples severally, all evidence was for homogamy, not complementarity. This direction of association was statistically significant for marrieds and for the total group.

But were they indeed measuring the same things as was Winch? Seven of the variables in the two studies were conceptually identical. The intervariable correlations as reported by Winch were rank ordered; ranks were also derived for the Schellenberg and Bee variables from the EPPS manual. The rank-order correlations between them were in the range .70 − .78 Half the remaining variance was attributable to the single need Nurturance, which was much more closely related to Succorance in the EPPS than in Winch.

More recently, Katz, Glucksberg, and Krauss (1960), using 56 couples with a mean marriage length of 5 years, incorporated EPPS data into Winch's husband–wife versus random pairs design. The results were overwhelmingly opposed to complementarity.

It is our judgment, in view of the foregoing discussion, that the complementary-need hypothesis as now stated is not tenable.

Due to cluster and factor analyses of his data (Ktsanes, 1955; Roos, 1957; Winch, Ktsanes, and Ktsanes, 1955), Winch believes at least two basic dimensions operate in marital patterning. He has labeled these *dominant–submissive* and *nurturant–receptive*. (One cannot fail to note the correspondence between the polarities and marital sex roles as ordinarily conceived.) Applying these dimensions to his case histories, he discovers the following generalizations which he then submits as hypotheses for verification. For example, irrespective of gender, individuals who are high in Nurturance tend to mate with those who are highly Receptive and relatively non-Nurturant; individuals who are high in Dominance mate with those who are high in Submissiveness and relatively non-Dominant. Schellenberg and Bee (1960) tested these hypotheses with what appear to be the relevant EPPS variables; the hypotheses were not confirmed. Yet Winch's case reports (Winch, 1958) are certainly convincing; and further, in analyzing his 25 couples, he reports the following distribution: marriages in which the husband is dominant, 13; in which the wife is dominant, 9; mixed dominance, 3. Not only Schellenberg and Bee, but also Lu (1952c) report a far greater proportion of equalitarian matings than Winch's couples exhibit.

A further consideration strikes the reader of Winch's case histories. "One is impressed with the degree to which it is the recollections the subject has of his parents (as he knew them between, say, 6 and 18) which either directly, or as a counter-process, shapes his needs" (Strodtbeck, 1959). And most impressive is the extent to which it is *both,* or the *cross*-sex rather than the like-sex parent who is emulated.

The suspicion grows that Winch's subjects are simply not typical of mate-selecting individuals. That they should be exceptional seems entirely reasonable, when one considers that they were drawn from a postwar, early marrying, GI Bill of Rights supported, campus group. Certainly one can take some exception to any researcher's subjects, and this review cannot stand on psychosocial speculations concerning these individuals. However, any reader of Winch's case histories must be impressed with how far these individuals veer from the generalizations proposed in this review as predictive of marital success. One would therefore predict an unusual degree of disharmony and unhappiness in these marriages. Perhaps follow-up data will some day be available by which the accuracy of these remarks may be judged.

Now if it be granted that the complementary-needs approach has not met with undue success, though making valuable contributions as to level of approach and research orientation, where has it gone awry? The answer to this question lies in developments observable in the entire enterprise of behavior analysis. The marriage relationship can be considered as a stimulus situation comprised of expectations specific to marriage. These marriage roles can thus be expected to order (or even assign) the operative needs of the individuals concerned. Assessment of needs not specific to marriage is clearly not the logical entre to predictive study.[3]

ROLE THEORY

The role-analysis approach to marriage research has had its advocates for many years.

> What the Freudians fail to recognize, and Mead left undeveloped, is the notion of multiple patterns of role-taking in response to the varied demands of the groups in which the individual aspires to membership (Mowrer and Mowrer, 1951, p. 30).

Kargman (1957) has argued for the efficacy of role analyses, as opposed to the intrapsychic approach, in enabling both counsellor and client to appreciate marriage-relationship problems. Earlier, Mangus has offered an elaboration or role theory as it may be applied to marriage counselling. He offers sample hypotheses, e.g., the integrative quality of a marriage is a function of role perception, role expectation, and role performance of marital partners. This paper, along with that of Sarbin, may well be read for expositions of general role theory (Mangus, 1957; Sarbin, 1954). Research in marriage roles was active by at least 1950.

The most sophisticated psychosocial treatment of marriage relationships now available is that of Parsons and Bales (1955), which consequently deserves a brief résumé here. Parsons demonstrates that in the processes of development, need dispositions, object relations, and identifications are inextricably related; so that although needs may certainly be considered as relatively enduring, as an individual finds himself engaged in a given social interaction, or assuming a given social role, this situation *organizes* (by differential orderings, rankings, and valences) the enduring need units. Any theory of action must deal not with the isolated units but with the role-ascribed organization of these units. Thus, "The role expectation . . . *is* itself also a motivational unit" (Parson and Bales, 1955, p. 107).

Parsons (Parsons and Bales, 1955) offers this pretty metaphor: "highly differentiated need-dispositions constitute a kind of "key-board." A given role-orientation is a "tune" played on that keyboard. Many different tunes will strike the same notes but in different combinations, and some will be altogether omitted from some tunes . . . the pattern of the tune is not deducible from the structure of the key-board (p. 171).

The two dominant *leit-motifs* are the male and female sex roles. Following an analysis of child socialization in terms of family structure, Parsons (Parsons and Bales, 1955) concludes:

If this general analysis is correct, then the most fundamental difference between the sexes in personality type is that, relative to the total culture as a whole, the masculine personality tends more to the predominance of instrumental interests, needs and functions, presumably in whatever social system both sexes are involved, while the feminine personality tends more to the primacy of expressive interests, needs and functions. We would expect, by and large, that other things being equal, men would assume more technical, executive, and "judicial" roles, women more supportive, integrative and "tension-managing" roles (p. 101).

These principles he then applies to marriage roles. In Parsons' system, there are two primary axes of personality differentiation, *power* and *instrumental–expressive*. In marriage, power equalization is the norm.[4] As to the instrumental expressive axis, ". . . the husband has the primary adaptive responsibilities, relative to the outside situation, and that internally he is in the first instance "giver-of-care," or pleasure, and secondarily the giver of love, whereas the wife is primarily the giver of love and secondarily the giver of care or pleasure" (Parsons and Bales, 1955, p. 151).

The husband-wife relationship is, of course, a subsystem of the family collectivity, which involves the performance of many roles. For example, the woman as mother must adopt instrumental primacy vis-à-vis her child, while the child in his role functions with expressive primacy. Obviously, the number, sex, and temperament of children which come to a couple must affect profoundly all dimensions of marital patterning and outcome. The limitations of this essay, however, allow no more than briefly noting this important caution (see Farber and Blackman, 1956).

Parsons' formulations are not simple, yet the level of complexity is appropriate to that of the phenomena. The theory has, however, outstripped research verification. It is our next task to review marriage-role researches, comparing their results to our own and to Parsons' generalizations.

In the first place, McGinnes (1958) repeated the study of Hill (1945) on campus values in mate selection. Subjects rated the importance to mate selection of 18 personal characteristics (emotional stability, good health, chastity, etc.). Remarkable consistency was demonstrated between the two studies, separated in time by 17 years. Shifts occurred principally in those items most clearly related to "companionate" marriages, and thus predictable from the generally-accepted view that marriages are shifting from "traditional" to "companionate" structuring. Role expectations, then, may be held to exhibit reasonable stability over time.

Shifts do, however, occur in individuals over time. Different patterns of traits—both those desired in the partner, and those believed to be important by the partner—are evident when subjects have reference to marriage partners than when reference is to dating partners (Hewitt, 1958). Marriage role expectations are held to differ according to courtship stage (Hobart, 1958).[5]

Occurring within a context of basic similarity, then, an individual's expectation shows differences according to the mate role in which he operates. The courtship is *somewhat* different than the marriage role. Parsons has predicted this difference, and suggests that it springs from need achievement, which operates forcefully through date selection and courtship, then much less saliently in marriage roles. It is impossible to verify this explanation with data now available, but the phenomenon of difference within basic similarity stands. It will be recalled that many dimensions, demonstrably involved in assortative mating, are found to occur intensified in more satisfactory marriages. A hypothesis for further investigation therefore offers itself; the greater the concordance between courtship and marriage role—that is, the less salient during courtship are those variables nonrelevant to marriage-roles (e.g., need achievement) —the greater the probability of marital success.

Investigations have been made of the effect of role disagreement on marriages. Jacobsen (1952) found that divorced couples exhibit a greater disparity in their attitudes toward the roles of husband and wife in marriage than do married couples. But Hobart and Klausner (1959) found no relationship between marital-role disagreement and marital satisfaction. The published examples from the questionnaires used in these two studies offer no opportunity for comparison as to equivalence. Neither study, however, used a random man–woman pairing control (or its equivalent) as should certainly be done

following Corsini (1956a, 1956b). Couch (1958) found con-
census on husband and wife roles to increase with length of
marriage, as did accuracy in assuming the role of the other
mate. The study, however, was cross-sectional rather than longitudinal. Couch offers it principally for its methodological and
conceptual interests, which it indeed possesses.

The most ambitious attempt to test Parsons' hypotheses has
been that of Farber (1957). The questions raised by this study
are many and important; adequate consideration requires a
somewhat detailed examination. Parsons and Bales (1955)
make the broad assignment of task-oriented roles to the husband, and socioemotional roles to the wife (each role being
subordinate to the common value system). Farber notes that
for the home-centered woman, and especially for the wife with
children, less opportunity for variation from the socioemotional
matrix is possible than is the case for the more mobile husband. Therefore, marriage integration is more dependent on
the husband's conformity to the wife's values than vice versa.
Farber uses three variables:

1. Marital Integration: measured by the number of times
husband and wife rate self or spouse as stubborn, gets angry
easily, feelings easily hurt, nervous or irritable, moody, jealous,
dominating or bossy, easily excited, easily depressed, and self-
centered.

2. Perceived Similarity between Self and Other: (husband
and wife, husband and child, wife and child, etc.) measures for
this variable are derived from the same ratings of the 10 traits
listed for Variable 1.

3. Socioemotional Valuation in Interaction: measured by
the following five values, which, along with others, were
ranked by subjects in order of importance: (*a*) "companionship," the family members feeling comfortable with each other
and being able to get along together; (*b*) "personality development," continued increase in family members' ability to understand and get along with people and to accept responsibility;
(*c*) "satisfaction" of family members "with amount of affection
shown," and of the husband and wife in their sex life; (*d*)

"emotional security," feeling that the members of the family really need each other emotionally and trust each other fully; and (e) "a home," having a place where the family members feel they belong, where they feel at ease, and where other people do not interfere in their lives.

From the foregoing, Farber hypothesizes:

1. The ranking of items relating to socioemotional aspects of interaction by wives tends to be higher than the ranking by their husbands.

2. The degree of marital integration varies directly with the ranks assigned by the husband to domestic values pertaining to socioemotional aspects of interaction.

Then, using 99 couples, trained interviewers, and ending in a dazzling (indeed sometimes blinding) display of mathematical manipulation, he accepts all four hypotheses as confirmed at the .05 level. But this study requires scrutiny. As for Hypothesis 1, Parsons' prediction of husband–wife differentiation in marriage roles along an instrumental–expressive axis is confirmed. But as for Hypothesis 2, when one examines the instruments used to measure the two variables involved, one concludes that it is demonstrated only that "husbands who are dedicated to getting along well in the family tend to occur in families which get along well." That is, marital integration is indexed by the same concept used to index socio-emotional role taking. Small wonder that they coincide.[6]

But this exception taken to Farber's design can also be taken to the majority of marital studies in the literature. For all the objective measures of marital satisfaction now current are heavily weighted with indices of togetherness, of agreement, of interpersonal smooth sailing. As a typical example, on the recently published Locke-Wallace short test (Locke and Wallace, 1959), 11 of the 15 items seem related to social emotional integration via agreement and togetherness. Certainly less friction in marriage may produce greater durability. Buerkle, Anderson, and Badgley (1961) have factor analyzed responses to Yale Marital Interaction Battery, composed of endorsements of alternative solutions to marital conflict situations. Factor scores were computed, and differences between adjusted marital groups and nonadjusted groups reported. The nonadjusted marriages were at that time being counseled for marital difficulties. The adjusted were marriages drawn from religion-affiliated groups. (The authors recognize the problem of accepting this group as adjusted.) At any rate, adjusted husbands were more likely to submit to wife domination and to grant the wife greater deference and respect. Adjusted wives were more likely to defer to the husband's judgment, and to expect less deference and respect from their husbands.

This study does not, however, speak to the issue of marital happiness. And, if considerations of "socioemotional integration" are less salient for the man in his marital role, it would seem that his marital happiness and success must be assessed by indices more pertinent to the satisfaction of his own peculiar motives.

We turn now to the important work of Langhorne and Secord (1955). When role expectations are analyzed separately for men and for women, in terms of *motivational units,* an impressive difference occurs; that is to say, women need different things from husbands than husbands need from wives. Langhorne and Secord have performed the service of describing, empirically, this difference. In six states (Virginia, Georgia, Mississippi, Ohio, Kansas, and Wyoming) 5,000 college and university students were asked to list, on blank paper, those traits which were desired in a mate. The authors then categorized (arbitrarily, but rather convincingly) the traits into need units adapted from Murray's list. Significant differences in need patterns did *not* occur by age, marital status, or geographical region. Differences by *sex* were significant both statistically and theoretically.

Women are more concerned than men with receiving affection, love, sympathy, and understanding from their spouse, although it should be recalled that (this) need is one of the strongest of both sexes. Secondly, males are more desirous of having a spouse who is neat and tidy about the home, and who will adjust to a routine, avoid friction, be even-tempered, home-loving, reasonable and dependable than are females. . . . Another category with a relatively large absolute difference is (*Social stimulus value*). Men are more concerned about the impression their future wife will make upon their friends and acquaintances than are women about the impression their future husband makes upon other persons. Women also stress (*Achievement*) more than males: in the present group not a single male listed an achievement trait as desirable in his future wife, whereas 6.8 per cent of the traits listed by women were in this category. Included here are such traits as getting ahead, ambitious, enjoys working, energetic, has high status profession, etc. (Langhorne and Secord, 1955, p. 32).

It is obvious that analysis is needed to determine if such grouped traits do indeed covary. However, Langhorne and Secord's groupings do no violence to customary conceptions of the need units employed. And their results are provocative. Not only does an individual wish the spouse to conform to the appropriate sex role, but notice particularly that heavily emphasized are those attributes which implement performance of the respondent's *own* role. The wife, whose role responsibility is socioemotional, wishes a husband who will work with her in an atmosphere of loving intimacy; the "instrumental" husband wishes a wife, who through her attractiveness and efficiency, implements his responsibility for instrumental success. This does not contradict the concomitant desires, respectively, for an achieving husband and for a loving wife.

Thus, following Parsons and Farber, we might indeed expect marital satisfaction to increase as the husband's socioemotional valuation increases. But for the wife, not necessarily for the husband whose marital satisfaction might be more reliably forecast by the degree to which his mate assists the performance of the male-instrumental expectations.

The obvious extension of this emerging generalization was made a decade ago by Ort (1950). His basic hypothesis is: "the amount of self-judgement of 'happiness' or 'unhappiness' in marriage depends upon, or is at least related to, the number of conflicts between role expectations and roles played by the subject, and role expectation for the subject's mate, and the roles played by the subject's mate, as the subject sees it." Fifty married couples were verbally queried on 22 issues, for example: Should a husband kiss his wife when he leaves for work? Should a husband expect to win most arguments? Both expectation concerning these roles and the subjects perception of the performances of them in the marriage were recorded. The number of conflicts between expectation and performance (for self and for mate) were totaled for each individual. Conflict totals correlated $-.83$ with subject's self-rating on a 10-point happiness scale.

Ort concludes that happiness lies in the individual playing the role he expects, and in having the spouse play the role expected of him or her, regardless of what these roles might be. "The author interviewed certain couples who entered marriage expecting to be sexually promiscuous and with those expectations fulfilled, their self-evaluation was number one. Likewise the author interviewed couples who had expected fidelity for the self and the mate and were fulfilling these expectations and they also gave themselves a happiness rating of number one" (Ort, 1950, p. 697).

As noted above, Hobart and Klausner (1959) found no relation between marital-role disagreement and marital satisfaction. In their study, 70 items of a role inventory (a mailed questionnaire) were endorsed from one through five, and role disagreement calculated through the sum of the 70 differences between spouses. These authors interpret their results as refuting Ort. Note however, that they did not investigate expectations *satisfied,* which is central to Ort's thinking.

Hurwitz (1959) has pursued the issue of expectation and satisfaction with his Index of Strain. Ten role items (e.g., "I am a companion to my wife") were ranked twice by each husband and each wife, first for the subject's performance, and second for the expectations of the spouse's behavior. The Index of Strain is the cube root of the sum of the cubes of the differences between the ranks the subjects assign to each role. Hurwitz reports the following results.

The Index of Strain is significantly higher for husbands than for wives. That is, wives conform more to husband's expectations than husbands do to wives'. The husbands' and wives' Index of Strain correlate $+.20$. The correlation of the Index of Strain with the Locke-Burgess-Cottrell Marital Adjustment Scale are as follows: the husband's Index of Strain is $-.22$ with their own marital adjustment, and $-.23$ with the wives' marital adjustment. Yet the wives' Index of Strain is significantly correlated with neither their own nor their husbands' adjustment!

This is another demonstration that the husband's is the key role in marital success. Though the relationships between expectation and satisfaction, even for husbands, are not as strong as in Ort's study, this must be in part attributable to the difference in the sample of role items.

Certainly satisfaction now seems related to happiness, perhaps tautologically. But satisfaction of what? Ort suggests role expectations. Katz, Glucksberg, and Krauss (1960) investigated some aspects of need satisfaction. Subjects rate the satisfaction provided by the mate on each of 11 EPPS variables. These satisfactions were also totaled for each subject. For wives, the totals were positively related to their own scores on Nurturance and Succorance; positively related to their husbands' scores on Nurturance and Achievement; and negatively to husbands' scores on Abasement and Autonomy. The totals for husbands were positively related to wives' scores on Succorance and Nurturance, and negatively to wives' Autonomy and Dominance. If any generalization can be drawn from these complex results, it would seem that individuals' needs are best satisfied within the marriage when both husband and wife operate with something like conventionally expected sex roles, modified by need constellations allowing companionate marriage structure.

One additional study, done early but infrequently cited, has attempted to assess need satisfaction's effect—in this case, on mate selection (Strauss, 1947). Three-hundred seventy-three engaged or recently married subjects checked items on a questionnaire, if these items described one of their major needs. Later, they were asked if the mate, or other persons, satisfied these needs. "Only 8.0% of the population appraised some other person as having satisfied their needs better than had the actual mate. As high a percentage as 89.2 appraised no other person of opposite sex as having filled major needs better than had the mate" (Strauss, 1947, p. 333). The distribution of needs satisfied appears to be highly skewed positively. This study deserves replication with adequate controls and an assessment technique which is less crude. But Strauss' study possesses the virtue of investigating needs appropriate to within-marriage considerations; for example, a need for "someone who shows me a lot of affection"; "who helps me in making important decisions"; "for someone who loves me."

The crucial issue now facing marriage-role researchers seems to be the identification of the crucial *dimensions* of marriage-role expectations and performances. These dimensions must be established through the observed covariation of discrete action units. The author is currently engaged in such an enterprise.

SUMMARY AND CONCLUSION

Let us now draw together summary generalizations from our study of existing research and theoretical materials.

Mates are selected from a field of eligibles. This field is determined by homogamy as to race, ethnic origin, social class, age, religion, and by residential propinquity. Exploration of this field is a function of unknown psychological variables. Cultural homogamys provide for a measure of similarity between mates with respect to social, value, and personality characteristics. Mate-selection (courtship) roles manifest patterns of needs and expectations which differ in content and organization from marriage roles. The greater the congruence between the two roles, the greater the likelihood of marital satisfaction. Modal role definitions exist, and are sex-differentiated. They are provided for by parental identifications. The husband role is the more instrumental, the wife role the more expressive–integrative. The wife being therefore more accommodating, the husband more rigid in role needs, the likelihood of marital success is a function of the husband's possession of the expected instrumental needs and capacities. Many individuals and marriages are not organized along these modal principles. The more general statement, therefore, is that marital satisfaction is a function of the satisfaction of needs and/or expectations specific to husband and wife roles.

The author recognizes that these are largely unverified hypotheses. They are, however, reasonably interrelated and made worthy of research effort by an existing body of data. This approach, however, has a serious limitation: it is largely restricted, by empirical data now available, to considerations of assortative mating and happiness in mating. Surely we must enlarge our view, in order, for example, to investigate developmental processes in marriage with Foote (1956), and psychological change processes with Uhr (1957).

Other reviewers might well abstract generalizations quite different from those presented here. Any analyst's eyes are focused by his own convictions, and the author's own might be made explicit here: role theory provides the best available framework for investigation of psychological phenomena in marriage; and, psychologists may well apply their skills to these issues—issues of pressing practical, ameliorative, and basic theoretical concern.

NOTES

1. Several of the assessments to be made here have adumbrations scattered through the literature and acknowledgments will be made below.
2. TAT-O disappears.
3. In a stimulating article, Rosow characterizes Winch's dichotomizations as "the operational assumption that people do not have *general* personality needs, but segregate these according to different social roles and gratify them on a role-specific basis; that is, some needs in one role and others in

92   *Psychological Patterning in Marriage*

another" (Rosow, 1957). However, there is nothing in published accounts
of the interviews which demonstrate that they were adequate for (or even
conceived so as to provide) marriage-role-specific assessment of needs;
further, neither hypotheses nor results are reported which give any
evidence of a within-without patterning or effect. We must agree, however,
to the extent that Winch's work contains the ungerminated seed of the
theoretical tree which we hope shall fructify in the following section.

4. Research seems to substantiate this assertion. Most marital partners see
power equally in their roles. As to the effects on power distribution of
extramarital role variations, e.g., working wives versus housewives, there
is disagreement (see Heer, 1958 versus Blood and Hamblin, 1958). But
the relationship between power-as-need and power-as-influence is unresolved in the literature. This is unsurprising, since the relationship of
motive to behavior constitutes a key dilemma in psychology. This
situation also highlights the importance of role-specified needs as a
construct, offering as it does a potential solution to this basic theoretical
issue.

5. Langhorne and Secord (1955) do not find ideal-mate conceptions differing
by age or marital statue. But their variables are need units (see below);
and do not appear comparable to these studies, which deal with specific
traits.

6. Farber also investigates other hypotheses. Inspection of the measuring
devices again demonstrates conceptual nonseparation of the independent
and dependent variables. Farber maintains that statistically, the indices
need not covary. However, identical thermomenters may also vary
independently; our point is that Farber has placed two thermometers in a
single solution.

REFERENCES

Blood, R. O., Jr., and Hamblin, R. L. The effect of the wife's employment on
the family power structure. *Soc. Forces,* 1958, *36,* 347–352.

Bowerman, C. E., and Day, Barbara R. A test of the theory of complementary
needs as applied to couples during courtship. *Amer. sociol. Rev.,* 1956, *21,*
602–605.

Bowman. C. C. Uncomplementary remarks on complementary needs. *Amer.
sociol. Rev.,* 1955, *20,* 466.

Buerkle, J. V., Anderson, T. R., and Badgley, R. F. Altruism, race conflict, and
marital adjustment: A factor analysis of marital interaction. *Marriage
fam. Liv.,* 1961, *23,* 20–26.

Burchinal, L. G., Hawkes, G. R., and Gardner, B. Personality characteristics
and marital satisfaction. *Soc. Forces,* 1957 *35,* 218–222.

Burgess, E. W., and Cottrell, L. *Predicting success or failure in marriage.*
Englewood Cliffs, N.J.: Prentice-Hall, 1939.

Burgess, E. W., and Wallin, P. *Engagement and marriage.* New York: Lippincott, 1953.

The major portion of this report was written at the University of Michigan and
supported by a United States Public Health Service fellowship. The author wishes to
express his gratitude to E. Lowell Kelly for his direction and encouragement.

Commins, W. D. Marriage age of oldest sons. *J. soc. Psychol.*, 1932, *3*, 487–490.

Corsini, R. J. Multiple predictors of marital happiness. *Marriage fam. Liv.*, 1956, *18*, 240–242.(a)

Corsini, R. J. Understanding and similarity in marriage. *J. abnorm. soc. Psychol.*, 1956, *52*, 327–332.(b)

Couch, C. J. The use of the concept "role" and its derivatives in a study of marriage. *Marriage fam. Liv.*, 1958, *20*, 353–357.

Dreikurs, R. The choice of a mate. *Int. J. indiv. Psychol.*, 1930, *1*, 103.

Dymond, Rosalind. Interpersonal perception and marital happiness. *Canad. J. Psychol.*, 1954, *8*, 164–171.

Farber, B. An index of marital integration. *Sociometry*, 1957, *20*, 117–133.

Farber, B., and Blackman, L. S. Marital role tensions and number and sex of children. *Amer. sociol. Rev.*, 1956, *21*, 596–601.

Fluegel, J. C. *Psychoanalytic study of the family*. London: Hogarth, 1926.

Foote, N. Matching of husband and wife in phases of development. In, *Transactions of the third world congress of sociology*. Vol. 4. London: International Sociological Association, 1956. Pp. 24–34.

Freud, S. Three essays on sexuality. *Complete psychological works*. Vol. 7. London: Hogarth, 1953.

Hamilton, G. V., and McGowan, C. *What is wrong with marriage?* New York: Albert & Charles Boni, 1930.

Heer, D. M. Dominance and the working wife. *Soc. Forces*, 1958, *36*, 341–347.

Hewitt, L. E. Student perceptions of traits desired in themselves as dating and marriage partners. *Marriage fam. Liv.*, 1958, *20*, 344–349.

Hill, R. Campus values in mate selection. *J. home Econ.*, 1945, *37*, 554–558.

Hobart, C. W. Some effects of romanticism during courtship on marriage role opinions. *Social. soc. Res.*, 1958, *42*, 336–343.

Hobart, C. W., and Klausner, W. J. Some social interactional correlates of marital role disagreement, and marital adjustment. *Marriage fam. Liv.*, 1959, *21*, 256–263.

Hollingshead, A. B. Cultural factors in the selection of marriage mates. *Amer. sociol. Rev.*, 1950, *15*, 619–627.

Hurwitz, N. The index of strain as a measure of marital satisfaction. *Sociol. soc. Res.*, 1959, *44*, 106–111.

Jacobsen, A. H. Conflict of attitudes toward the roles of husband and wife in marriage. *Amer. sociol. Rev.*, 1952, *17*, 146–150.

Kagan, J. The concept of identification. *Psychol. Rev.*, 1958, *65*, 296–305.

Kargman, Marie W. The clinical use of social system theory in marriage counseling. *Marriage fam. Liv.*, 1957, *19*, 263–269.

Katz, A. M., and Hill, R. Residential propinquity and marital selection: A review of theory, method, and fact. *Marriage fam. Liv.*, 1958, *20*, 27–335.

Katz, I., Glucksberg, S., and Krauss, R. Need satisfaction and Edwards PPS scores in married couples. *J. consult. Psychol.*, 1960, *24*, 203–208.

Kelly, E. L. Psychological factors in assortative mating. *Psychol. Bull.*, 1940 *37*, 576.

Kelly, E. L. Marital compatibility as related to personality traits of husbands and wives as rated by self and spouse. *J. soc. Psychol.*, 1941, *13*, 193–198.

Kephart, W. M. Some knowns and unknowns in family research: A sociological critique. *Marriage fam. Liv.*, 1957, *19*, 7–15.

Kernodle, W. Some implications of the homogamy-complementary needs theories of mate selection for sociological research. *Soc. Forces*, 1959, *38*, 145–152.

Kirkpatrick, C. A statistical investigation of psychoanalytic theory of mate selection. *J. abnorm. soc. Psychol.*, 1937, *32,* 427–430.

Ktsanes, T. Mate selection on the basis of personality type: A study utilizing an empirical typology of personality. *Amer. sociol. Rev.*, 1955, *20,* 547–551.

Ktsanes, T., and Ktsanes, Virginia. The theory of complementary needs in mate-selection. In R. F. Winch (Ed.), *Selected studies in marriage and the family.* New York: Holt, 1953. Pp. 435–453.

Langhorne, M. C., and Secord, P. F. Variations in marital needs with age, sex, marital status, and regional location. *J. soc. Psychol.*, 1955, 41, 19–37.

Locke, H. J., and Wallace, K. M. Short marital-adjustment and prediction tests: Their reliability and validity. *Marriage fam. Liv.*, 1959, *21,* 251–255.

Lu, Y.-C. Marital roles and marital adjustment. *Sociol. soc. Res.*, 1952, *36,* 364–368. (a)

Lu, Y.-C. Parent-child relations and marital roles. *Amer. sociol. Rev.*, 1952, *17,* 357–361. (b)

Lu, Y.-C. Parental role and parent-child relationships. *Marriage fam. Liv.*, 1952, *14,* 294–297. (c)

Lu, Y.-C. Predicting roles in marriage. *Amer. J. Sociol.*, 1952, *58,* 51–55. (d)

Luckey, Eleanor B. An investigation of the concepts of the self, mate, parents, and ideal in relation to degree of marital satisfaction. *Dissert. Abstr.*, 1959, *20,* 396–397.

Luckey, Eleanor B. Marital satisfaction and congruent self-spouse concepts. *Soc. Forces,* 1960, 39, 153–157. (a)

Luckey, Eleanor B. Marital satisfaction and parent concepts. *J. consult. Psychol.*, 1960, *24,* 195–204. (b)

McGinnes, R. Campus values in mate-selection: A repeat study. *Soc. Forces,* 1958, *36,* 368–373.

Mangus, A. Relation between the young woman's conceptions of her intimate male associates and of her ideal husband. *J. soc. Psychol.*, 1936, *7,* 403–420.

Mangus, A. Role theory and marriage counseling. *Soc. Forces,* 1957, 35, 200–209.

Meyer, Carol T. Complementarity and marital conflict. *Dissert. Abstr.*, 1957, *17,* 20 82.

Motz, Annabelle B. The role conception inventory: A tool of research in social psychology. *Amer. sociol. Rev.*, 1952, *17,* 465–471.

Mowrer, E. R., and Mowrer, Harriet. The social psychology of marriage. *Amer. sociol. Rev.*, 1951, *16,* 27–36.

Ort, R. S. A study of role-conflicts as related to happiness in marriage. *J. abnorm. soc. Psychol.*, 1950, *45,* 691–699.

Parsons, T. and Bales R. F. *Family, socialization and interaction process.* Glencoe, Ill.: Free Press, 1955.

Payne, D. E., and Mussen, P. H. Parent-child relations and father identification among adolescent boys. *J. abnorm. soc. Psychol.*, 1956, *52,* 358–363.

Preston, M. G., Peltz, W. L., Mudd, Emily H., and Froscher, Hazel B. Impressions of personality as a function of marital conflict. *J. abnorm. soc. Psychol.*, 1952, *47,* 326–336.

Rogers, C. R., and Dymond, Rosalind F. *Psychotherapy and personality change.* Chicago: Univer. Chicago Press, 1954.

Roos, D. E. Complementary needs in mate selection: A study based on R-type factor analysis. *Dissert. Abstr.*, 1957, *17,* 426.

Rosow, I. Issues in the concept of need-complementarity. *Sociometry,* 1957, *20,* 216–233.

Sarbin, T. R. Role theory. In G. Lindsay (Ed.), *Handbook of social psychology.* Vol. 1. Cambridge: Addison-Wesley, 1954. Pp. 223–255.

Schellenberg, J. A., and Bee, L. S. A reexamination of the theory of complementary needs in mate-selection. *Marriage fam. Liv.,* 1960, *22,* 227–232.

Sears, R. *Survey of objective studies of psychoanalytic concepts.* New York: Social Science Research Council, 1942.

Strauss, A. The ideal and the chosen mate. *Amer. J. Sociol.,* 1946, *52,* 204–208. (a)

Strauss, A. The influence of parent-images upon marital choice. *Amer. sociol. Rev.,* 1946, *11,* 554–559. (b)

Strauss, A. Personality needs and marital choice. *Soc. Forces,* 1947, *25,* 332–339.

Strodtbeck, F. L. A review of mate-selection: A study of complementary needs. *Amer. sociol. Rev.,* 1959, *24,* 437–438.

Terman, L. M. *Psychological factors in marital happiness.* New York: McGraw-Hill, 1938.

Terman, L. M., and Butterwiser, P. Personality factors in marital compatibility. I. *J. soc. Psychol.,* 1935, *6,* 143–171.

Terman, L. M., and Butterwiser, P. Personality factors in marital compatibility. II. *J. soc. Psychol.,* 1935, *6,* 267–289.

Terman, L. M., and Oden, M. H. *The gifted child grows up.* Stanford: Stanford Univer. Press, 1947.

Uhr, L. M. Personality changes during marriages. Unpublished doctoral dissertation, University of Michigan, 1957.

Winch, Martha. Some implications in marital counseling. In R. F. Winch (Ed.), *Mate selection.* New York: Harper, 1958. Pp. 310–329.

Winch, R. F. *The modern family.* New York: Holt, 1952.

Winch, R. F. The theory of complementary needs in mate-selection: Final results on the test of general hypotheses. *Amer. sociol. Rev.,* 1955, *20,* 552–555. (a)

Winch, R. F. The theory of complementary needs in mate selection: A test of one kind of complementariness. *Amer. sociol. Rev.,* 1955, *20,* 52–56. (b)

Winch, R. F. Comment on "A test of the theory of complementary needs as applies to couples during courtship" by Bowerman and Day. *Amer. sociol. Rev.,* 1957, *22,* 336.

Winch, R. F. *Mate-selection: A study of complementary needs.* New York: Harper, 1958.

Winch, R. F., Ktsanes, T., and Ktsanes, Virginia. The theory of complementary needs in mate-selection: An analytic and descriptive study. *Amer. sociol. Rev.,* 1954, *19,* 241–249.

Winch, R. F., Ktsanes, T., and Ktsanes, Virginia. Empirical elaboration of the theory of complementary needs in mate-selection. *J. abnorm. soc. Psychol.,* 1955, *51,* 509–513.

Winch, R. F., and More, D. M. Does the TAT add information to interviews?: Statistical analysis of the increment. *J. clin. Psychol.,* 1956, *12,* 316–321. (a)

Winch, R. F., and More, D. M. Quantitative analysis of qualitative data in the assessment of motivation: Reliability, congruence, and validity. *Amer. J. Sociol.,* 1956, *61,* 445–452. (b)

3 Note on Need Complementarity in Marriage

GEORGE LEVINGER

Tharp's (1963) recent review of studies on the psychological patterning in marriage presents incisive observations about knowledge in this area. His comments on hypotheses and on findings are extremely useful.

It seems necessary, though, to supplement his discussion of Winch's hypothesis on complementary needs in mate selection. To quote Tharp (1963), "In marriage research, no other hypothesis produced in the last decade has been as influential [p. 107]." Yet, after 3 pages of methodological critique of Winch's study, Tharp concludes "the complementary-need hypothesis as now stated is untenable [p. 110]."

This writer agrees with Tharp's general conclusion. Never-

From *Psychological Bulletin*, Vol. 61, No. 2, 1964, pp. 153–157. Copyright 1964 by the American Psychological Association. The writer's concern with these issues has arisen in the course of research on marital interaction, supported largely by Grant M-4653 from the National Institute of Mental Health, United States Public Health Service. Discussions with Barbara Allan, who is doing empirical research related to the hypothesis, have been helpful.

theless, in order to understand why the evidence in favor of Winch's hypothesis is thus far of dubious quality, it is important to go beyond pointing at methodological weaknesses in existing studies. One must also examine the conceptual issues that are involved.

Three issues to which little previous notice has been drawn are the following ones. 1. There exists a logical confusion in the accepted conceptual distinction between *complementarity* and *similarity* of needs. 2. There exists no explicit theoretical basis for deciding *which needs are complementary with which others,* and existing studies are obscure in their basis of selecting such need pairs. 3. The conceptual distinction between *internal* and *external* sources of need satisfaction has been ignored operationally in most research studies that ostensibly bear on the complementarity hypotheses.[1]

The significance of the need-complementarity hypothesis has been recognized not only by those interested in marriage and family relationships, but also by other social psychologists concerned with interpersonal behavior in general (e.g., Newcomb, 1956; Schutz, 1958; Thibaut and Kelley, 1959). From a theoretical standpoint, it is only reasonable to expect that the more Person A wants to give what Person B wants to receive (and the more B wants to give what A wants to receive), the easier it will be for the pair to form and to maintain a viable relationship. The more that such conditions exist, the greater will be the mutual reward of the pair members and the lower their cost of achieving it (Thibaut and Kelley, 1959).

1. The Distinction between Complementarity and Similarity: Complementarity may be defined as "mutually supplying each other's lack," or "serving to fill out or complete" (Webster's, 1946). Many of the most productive human relationships are complementary ones: male and female in the sex act, seller and buyer in the exchange, and so forth, In most examples that one can think of, the parts that "complete" the relationship are different in either quality or quantity. And this has given rise to the belief—either implicitly or explicitly expressed in the marriage literature—that complementarity

and similarity are mutually exclusive attributes of interpersonal relationships.

Let us examine Winch's definition of complementarity. If two persons, *A* and *B*, are interacting, the resulting gratifications of both are considered "complementary" if one of the following conditions is satisfied (Winch, Ktsanes, and Ktsanes, 1954):

Type I: "the need or needs in *A* which are being gratified are very *different in intensity* from the same needs in *B* which are also being gratified [p. 243]."

Type II: "the need or needs in *A* which are being gratified are *different in kind* from the need or needs being gratified in *B* [p. 243]."

According to Winch and his colleagues, if *A* is high on need Dominance and *B* low on this same need, Type I complementarity would occur. They also assert that Type II complementarity would arise where *A* is high on need Dominance and *B* high on need Deference or on need Abasement.

The above definition presents some sufficient conditions for a complementary relationship, but it omits other such conditions. Thereby, it leads one erroneously to the conclusion that if *A*'s and *B*'s needs differ *neither* in kind *nor* in intensity, then the relationship is not complementary.

Once apprehended, the error of this impression is clearly demonstrable. Let us assume the existence of a person, the perfect embodiment of Aristotle's ethical men, all of whose needs exist in perfect moderation. His need scores, on whatever scale one might care to use, fall exactly at the midpoint of the continuum. If Winch's definition were adequate, one would have to conclude that none of this man's needs could be complemented, since needs of *different* intensity would be either too high or too low. Such a conclusion seems untenable.

More tenable is the idea that *A*'s and *B*'s needs, *same* in kind and *equal* in intensity, will complement one another properly when both members of the pair possess the need in *moderate* quantity. Table 1 illustrates the point for Type I complementarity of the need for Dominance.

The implications of this reformation are both conceptual and methodological. Regarding the former, it is advisable that this important hypothesis be securely anchored to a sound logical footing. Until that is done, fruitful research on this subject would be rather difficult to recognize.

Concerning the latter, one may briefly observe that the so-called negative findings in studies of the need-complementarity hypothesis (e.g., Bowerman and Day, 1956; Katz, Glucksberg, and Krauss, 1960; Schellenberg and Bee, 1960) cannot be considered negative merely on the basis of low correlations between partners' needs of the same kind (ignoring for the moment the relation between needs of a different kind). For any given need, if *in general* both partners should indicate it in moderate intensity, then the correlation between the partners' amounts would be reduced artificially to zero, and yet there would be complementarity indeed.

2. Instances of Hypothesized Complementarity: Whereas the first issue is a relatively simple matter of logic, the second is a more complex conceptual and empirical matter. It concerns the question of where the domain of complementarity exists. For what needs can either Type I or Type II complementarity be postulated?

It seems sensible to say that need for Dominance is a case of Type I complementarity; that is, that two partners are better off when one of them needs to make influence attempts and the other to accept them. However, it is much harder to understand the grounds on which Winch, Ktsanes, and Ktsanes (1954) hypothesize Type I complementarity for other needs, such as need Achievement; it is obscure why A and B would be better off when one is high and the other low on need Achievement, as opposed to both being either high or low. For a maximal coordination of their efforts, maximum similarity of achievement motivation might well be most advisable.

It is also obscure how Winch, Ktsanes, and Ktsanes (1954) reason about Type II complementarity. For example, they hypothesize that Abasement–Hostility and Abasement–Nurturance are both complementary need pairs (p. 246). Winch's published work does not provide a clear theoretical rationale for enabling one to decide what kind of complementarity might be asserted for what kind of need under what conditions.

A more explicit approach toward this problem occurs in Schutz' (1958) more limited theory of need compatibility. Schutz confines his concern to three dimensions of need— inclusion, control, affection—all specifically *interpersonal* needs. While confining himself purely to instances of Type I need complementarity, Schutz distinguishes carefully between *A*'s wishing to *express* behavior and wishing to *receive* behavior along any given dimension. Concerning need for Control, for example, *A*'s and *B*'s needs are defined as compatible to the degree that (*a*) *A* wishes to *express* the same amount of control toward *B* that *B* wishes to *receive*, and also (*b*) to the degree that *A* wishes to *receive* the amount that *B* wishes to *express*.

Schutz not only presents a useful definition of several kinds of compatibility, but he also has offered some formulae for deriving meaningful scores on need compatibility, together with operations indicated by FIRO-B (Schutz, 1958).[2] So far, only one study of mate selection has reported the use of Schutz' instruments (Kerckhoff and Davis, 1962), but its results lend some support to a hypothesis of need complementarity. It was found that, for pairs of college students who had dated each other longer than 18 months, couples with high need complementarity on Schutz' dimensions made more "progress" in their courtship than couples low in such complementarity.

3. Internal versus External Sources of Need Gratification: The third issue refers to the source of satisfaction of any person's needs. An implicit assumption in marriage studies is that need-fit pertains primarily to the marital relationship itself. Yet marriage involves more than a personal relationship between two individuals. The partners are simultaneously involved, both individually and as a couple, in interactional situations in the external environment. There is a substitutability of sources of need gratification for each person's needs. Proverbi-

ally, it is accepted that the man whose dominance needs are frustrated at the office comes home to release his anger on wife, child, or dog. Or, conversely, the henpecked husband at home goes out to work to boss his employees. It is by no means necessary that individuals use the same pattern of need gratification within and outside the marital relationship.

Although Winch, Ktsanes, and Ktsanes, (1954) mentioned the distinction between need gratification "within the marriage" versus that "in all other situations," this distinction is unclear in their own published data analyses (e.g., Winch, 1958). Furthermore, in the work of other researchers (Bowerman and Day, 1956; Blazer, 1963; Katz, Glucksberg, and Krauss, 1960; Schellenberg and Bee, 1960), the distinction is almost entirely ignored. The latter studies, in employing the Edwards Personal Preference Schedule (Edwards, 1953), used a need measure specifically designed to measure needs in the general environment of the college student's peers. Their negative findings merely demonstrate, therefore, that marriage partners do not show any consistent correlation between such *general* needs. These studies can hardly claim to test the complementarity of these needs in the specific *marriage* situation.

Parenthetically, it is interesting to note that when Katz, Glucksberg, and Krauss, (1960) rewrote the Edwards Personal Preference Schedule items describing *general* need for Nurturance and need for Succorance to pertain *specifically* to spouse relations, they obtained their most significant findings for complementarity. Until investigators take account of this issue more directly in their measurement of specific needs, there will be no further evidence to support the original hypothesis by Winch and his colleagues.

This note has attempted to illuminate certain additional issues concerning the need-complementarity hypothesis, omitted in Tharp's (1963) review of marriage research. In this writer's opinion, the hypothesis, when properly conceived and operationalized, does have a viability that gives promise for continued study.[3]

NOTES

1. Some other important conceptual issues pertaining to need complementarity have been treated by Rosow (1957).
2. One difficulty in Schutz' approach is that his test refers only to the respondent's general peer reactions. As presently constituted, his measure is not appropriate for use with married couples; and is more difficult to translate adequately than, say, the items of the Edwards Personal Preference Schedule (Edwards, 1953).
3. While this paper was in press, additional evidence concerning the effects of *one kind* of need complementarity on marital interaction has been published (Katz, Cohen, & Castiglione, 1963).

REFERENCES

Blazer, J. A. Complementary needs and marital happiness. *Marriage fam. Liv.*, 1963, 25, 89–95.

Bowerman, C. E., and Day, Barbara R. A test of the theory of complementary needs as applied to couples during courtship. *Amer. sociol. Rev.*, 1956, *21*, 602–605.

Edwards, A. L. *Manual for the Edwards Personal Preference Schedule.* New York: Psychological Corporation, 1953.

Katz, I., Cohen, M., and Castiglione, L. Effect of one type of need complementarity on marriage partners' conformity to one another's judgments. *J. abnorm. soc. Psychol.*, 1963, *67*, 8–14.

Katz, I., Glucksberg, S., and Krauss, R. Need satisfaction and Edwards PPS scores in married couples. *J. consult. Psychol.*, 1960, *24*, 205–208.

Kerckhoff, A. C., and Davis, K. E. Value consensus and need complementarity in mate selection. *Amer. sociol. Rev.*, 1962, *27*, 295–303.

Newcomb, T. M. The prediction of interpersonal attraction. *Amer. Psychologist*, 1956, *11*, 575–586.

Rosow, I. Issues in the concept of need-complementarity. *Sociometry*, 1957, *20*, 216–233.

Schellenberg, J. A., and Bee, L. S. A reexamination of the theory of complementary needs in mate-selection. *Marriage fam. Liv.*, 1960, *22*, 227–232.

Schutz, W. C. *FIRO' A three-dimensional theory of interpersonal behavior.* New York: Rinehart, 1958.

Tharp, R. G. Psychological patterning in marriage. *Psychol. Bull.*, 1963, *60*, 97–117.

Thibaut, J. W., and Kelley, H. H. *The social psychology of groups.* New York: Wiley, 1959.

Webster's collegiate dictionary. (5th ed.) Springfield, Mass.: G.& C. Merriam, 1946.

Winch, R. F. *Mate-selection: A study of complementary needs.* New York: Harper, 1958.

Winch, R. F., Ktsanes, T., and Ktsanes, Virginia. The theory of complementary needs in mate-selection: An analytic and descriptive study. *Amer. sociol. Rev.*, 1954, *19*, 241 249.

4 *Reply to Levinger's Note*

ROLAND G. THARP

Levinger's "Note on Need Complementarity in Marriage" has performed the valuable service of clarifying the conceptual basis on which the social–psychological construct of need complementarity rests. His own reformulation takes account of more permutations than does Winch's system, and he has demonstrated that those who would pair people on the basis of *needs* must take account of complementarity, similarity, difference, compatibility, etc. In addition, he points out that no theoretical basis exists whereby needs may be paired, and we are agreed that attempted pairings have failed to predict social-psychological events.

Thus Levinger has brandished the knife of conceptual clarity, and in the process, committed euthanasia. For he has enabled us to see that a complementary-need hypothesis can

From *Psychological Bulletin*, Vol. 61, No. 2, 1964, pp. 158–160. Copyright 1964 by the American Psychological Association.

only state, in effect, that *some* combinations of *some* needs in *some* pattern of quantity and quality will eventuate in something satisfactory. And since there is as yet no convincing empirical support for *any* such combination, the CN hypothesis remains but a vague faith.

This faith is, I believe, based on the common-sense assumption that some sorts of people combine into more lasting, productive, and mutually satisfying groupings than would other people. Of course. That it should be otherwise is inconceivable. But should we assume that this matching is on the basis of motives? Levinger argues that the CN hypothesis is viable when needs *specific to the marriage situation* are under investigation. Far from omitting this issue, my original paper (Tharp, 1963b) states that "assessment of needs not specific to marriage is clearly not the logical entree to predictive study [p. 108]." Levinger and I are agreed that the constructs under scrutiny must be *role specific*.

The methodological ramifications of this position are as follows. The concept "role" pertains to expectations, perceptions, and actions specific to a particular situation. Thus it is inappropriate, in social-psychological research, to continue the very operations traditionally employed to assess needs. To abstract response tendencies to a wide variety of stimuli (whether questionnaire items or ambiguous pictures) necessarily brings a loss of the precision required to predict to a specific role.

But the more serious challenge to the CN hypothesis should be made on the basis of the constructs which it attempts to order. We must take account of specific stimulus situations, rather than attempt to predict from "stable" intraorganismic states. This is a development apparent in the entire enterprise of behavior analysis. Let us consider several examples, the first from the area of social psychology, in which examination of stable traits have given way to a closer inspection of specific conditions:

"The conception of leaders as people who possess certain distinctive traits has not proved to be satisfactory. A 'new view' or leadership is emerging which stresses the performance of needed functions and adaptability to changing situations. According to this conception, groups are (or should be) flexible in assigning leadership functions to various members as conditions change (Cartwright and Zander, 1960, p. 492).

As another example, in learning theory, drive state (motive, need) was once held accountable as a principal multiplicative constituent of predictive equations; or as the "organizer" of guiding internal stimulation sequences. Current statistical learning theory considers drive inducing operations to affect only the make-up of the stimulus set, the rate of sampling of stimulus set elements, or the probability that any one element will be sampled on any single trial (Estes, 1959).

The most radical statement of this movement toward stimuli is found, of course, in operant theory, where all internal states are extirpated from explanatory statements. Because of the organism's reinforcement history, the appearance of a discriminative stimulus results in a response. Thus the stimulus itself is motivating.

Other areas of psychological theory have profited from greater emphasis on stimulus situation, however, without abandoning their traditional concern with cognitions, perceptions, and expectations. In personality theory, the classical psychoanalytic position of heavy concentration on instinctual drive as the determiner of the form of individual behavior is undergoing steady revision. The neo-Freudians, the ego psychologists, and more recently Schachtel in his treatment of the allocentric mode of perception, have demonstrated that the most satisfying and productive human experiences are not to be found in need-dominated behavior but in the appropriate transactions with fully apprehended objects and situations (Schachtel, 1959).

As yet another example, consider the phenomenological approach to man; phenomenology would appear to be the antithesis of operant theory, yet the two are in basic agreement as to the necessity for greater concentration on stimulus conditions rather than on internal states "[The psychologist] never learns to know the *subject* better than by going to the *objects,* to the things of his world . . . the relationship of man to world is so profound, that it is an error to separate them . . . . Who wants to describe man should make an analysis of the 'landscape' within which he demonstrates, explains and reveals himself" (van den Berg, 1955, p. 32).

Let us then profit from the common experience of our colleagues. It is entirely conceivable that a man or woman is spurred to action as spouse by stimuli which are not operative in these individuals' lives as bartender or secretary. The first order of business for marriage research is the specification of the stimuli: what *is* it to be a spouse? We must be able to describe and quantify the various expectations, reciprocations, rights, and obligations which comprise the situation of spouse-hood (Tharp, 1963a). Perhaps some facets of this role structure will turn out to be complementary; it is more likely that some will, and others will not. But before concerning ourselves with patterning of elements, we had best identify the elements themselves.

These issues are no different in marriage research than in the investigation of any social group. We will be closer to knowing why some people form better groups than other people, when we are sure what the groups do, and when, and how.

REFERENCES

Cartwright, D., and Zander, A. *Group dynamics.* (2nd ed.) Evanston, Ill.: Row, Peterson, 1960.

Estes, W. K. The statistical approach to learning theory. In S. Koch (Ed.), *Psychology' A study of a science.* Vol. 2. *General systematic formulations, learning, and special processes.* New York: McGraw-Hill, 1959. Pp. 380–492.

Schachtel, E. G. *Metamorphosis.* New York: Basic Books, 1959.

Tharp, R. G. Dimensions of marriage roles. *Marriage fam. Liv.,* 1963, in press. (a)

Tharp, R. G. Psychological patterning in marriage. *Psychol. Bull.,* 1963, 60, 97–115. (b)

van den Berg, J. H. *The phenomenological approach to psychiatry.* Springfield, Ill.: Charles C. Thomas, 1955.

5

Blue-Collar Families

MIRRA KOMAROVSKY

Ever since it begun the world's bin growin' hasn't it? Things hev happened, things have bin discovered, people have bin thinking and improving and inventing but what do we know about it all?

—Beatie, the working-class rebel of *Roots*,
ARNOLD WESKER

President Johnson's war on poverty, the Manpower Development and Training Acts, the Area Redevelopment Act, and other legislation in recent years have drawn unprecedented attention to the poor—the deprived ethnic and racial minorities, and the unemployed in depressed areas. Before the poor had become a national preoccupation, family sociologists had made hundreds of studies of the college educated middle classes in our society. Yet little heed is paid those

From *Columbia University Forum*, Fall 1964, pp. 29–32. This chapter is adapted from *Blue-Collar Marriage*, New York: Random House, 1964.

in the socioeconomic stratum between these two groups—the stable, employed semiskilled manual or blue-collar wage earners who live above the subsistence level and are free of the disadvantages of racial and ethnic minorities, but who have little in the way of formal education.

William Jovanovich wrote in *The Saturday Review* (July 18, 1964) that "the working class as a proportionately large and socially identifiable segment of our society is all but disappearing" and that "the generic middle class now includes skilled and semiskilled laborers." Earlier than that, the United States Department of Labor asserted ("How American Buying Habits Change," 1959) that "the wage earner's way of life is well-nigh indistinguishable from that of his salaried cocitizens. Their homes, their cars, their babysitters, the style of the clothes their wives and children wear, the food they eat, the bank where they establish credit, their days off . . . all of these are alike and are becoming more nearly identical."

Is it a valid assumption that because blue-collar workers have acquired the buying habits of the salaried middle class, the way of life for both has become the same? Can we assume that a spread in patterns of "having" has been accompanied by a spread in ways of thinking, in values and attitudes? I do not think we can. I have recently completed, under a grant from the National Institute of Mental Health, a sociological study of blue-collar families, and I shall here record some of my impressions, especially as they contrast with those gained in my earlier studies among the college-educated.

For the study, 60 working-class couples were interviewed about their marriages—their ideals and expectations, their sexual relations, the marriage dialogue, the nature of friendship between the spouses, the differences between masculine and feminine roles, and ties with their relatives. Most of the couples interviewed were white Protestant and born of native parents. The average husband was a semiskilled worker in his early thirties, had less than a high school education, and earned wages of approximately $80 a week. He and his wife had three children. They lived in an industrial community about 15 miles from an Eastern metropolis.

The physical scene in which the blue-collar workers live is familiar enough. The homes are pleasant, if modest by middle-class standards; they are decorated with modern furniture and equipped with washing machines and television sets. But the intangible realm of values and attitudes is reminiscent of the past, for the blue-collar world is insulated from contemporary currents of thought. For example, in this age when even the children in middle-class families of college-educated parents prattle about inferiority complexes and mother fixations, the blue-collar parents have retained a pre-Freudian innocence about human behavior. Their concepts of child-rearing are few and simple. If they puzzle over the rebelliousness or disobedience of their children, they seek the explanation in discipline, and wonder if they have been "too easy" with one who is rebellious; if that explanation fails, they decide it is because "he has his father's temper."

Incidentally, it is often alleged that the psychological advances of the twentieth century have robbed college-educated parents of self-confidence. College-educated parents do, in fact, report more frequent feelings of inadequacy than uneducated parents. But my respondents are far from complacent. Mothers worry about their irritability and say, "It's real hard to know what to do; I shake and beat them and then I feel lousy." As a rule, they have not discovered Dr. Spock, and their guide is still the grandmother. The goals of child-rearing are expressed in moral terms: "To bring up kids in a respectable manner, to live a decent life, honest and true." They do not speak of "emotional security," "creativity," "capacity to grow," or of "relating to others." These ideas, which middle-class parents get from college courses and child psychologists, from the magazines they read and the social gatherings they attend, have not yet reached the average blue-collar worker. As the interviews progressed, I felt further and further removed from the world of the twentieth century—transported as if by a Wellsian time machine into an older era.

For me perhaps the most surprising aspect of the blue-collar world had to do not with manners and morals, but with the cognitive style of the people. The interviews, which took six hours each, were meant to focus on psychological relationships, but the respondents almost without exception thought in terms of the situational and material conditions of life. My impressions coincide with those of the British observer Richard Hoggart, author of *The Uses of Literacy,* who wrote that the essence of working-class life is the " 'dense and concrete' life, a life whose main stress is on the sensory, the detailed . . . [and] is characterized by a low level of abstraction." To the standard question "Does your husband have any favorites among the children?" my respondents frequently answered, "No; if he gets something for one kid, he always brings something for the other." "Think back over the past week or two. Has your husband done anything that hurt your feelings, made you mad, surprised you?" The word "surprise" was usually taken to mean an unexpected present. The word "help" meant money or services, not help in the psychological sense. "When you feel that way [low for no apparent reason] can your mother help you?" The woman might pause for a moment, being puzzled by the *non sequitur,* and say, "No, she doesn't have any cash to spare."

The interviewer had no need for parrying phrases to deflect the interview from himself to the respondent. College-educated men and women in similar interviews frequently intersperse their talk with such questions as "Don't you agree?" or "Don't you think that was unfair?" They appear to be telling their story and at the same time listening to it. They are concerned with the interviewer's reaction and make self-conscious remarks such as "Don't get me wrong," or "I guess I make him seem selfish." College-educated respondents are concerned not only with the interviewer's moral judgment, but also with the accuracy of his understanding. Realizing that behavior may result from a variety of motives, they are quick to anticipate and correct possible misconceptions.

In contrast, only a few of the working-class men and women exhibited this psychological subtlety and self-consciousness. That is not to say, of course, that they opened their hearts to an interviewer without guile or reticence. But whatever they were disposed to tell, they told flatly, without punctuating the narrative with asides. A woman when asked whether her husband was easy or difficult to talk to replied, "I can tell him anything I need to say." She did not perceive that the question might lend itself to qualifications; refinements had to be brought out by painstaking inquiry. The days may be full of joy and resentment, pity and pride, anger and love, boredom and frustration, but these emotions are not labeled, distinguished, or reflected upon. The charge is often made in this "age of self-awareness" that family life in the middle class suffers from the constant scrutiny of motivations and that the endless flow of words quenches genuine feeling and spontaneity. Nothing of the kind threatens the blue-collar families.

It is said further of middle-class couples that they are troubled by ambiguity of marriage roles; that neither mate is sure of what he may ask of the other or demand of himself. Should a husband be expected to help with the dishes or to take turns during the night with the baby's bottle? For working-class couples there is no issue over who does what around the house. Not only the men, but even the women, accept the traditional division of masculine and feminine tasks, and the women do not expect assistance from their husbands in everyday circumstances. Moreover, whereas educated women have misgivings about being "just a housewife," not a trace of this attitude appears in the blue-collar class. Attempts to tap feelings about the domestic role evoke a puzzled, "Why, it's regular, isn't it? It can't be anything else." Contrast this simple acceptance of a woman's status with the soul-searching of a college senior of my acquaintance who wrote on the eve of her marriage: "When I get married I want to be a homemaker and raise a family. But I foresee some possible conflicts. I wonder whether it will be difficult to adjust my ego to being just a housewife; I may feel guilty because I do not use my college education in some occupation. I wonder whether I will be intellectually stimulating to my husband. My mother's unfortunate experience adds to my fears; she is bored and lacks direction now that her children are grown."

How unself-conscious does the working-class wife appear with her simple view of her place when compared with my college friend. The one is exposed to the diverse ideas of family, school, and reading, and will never possess her blue-collar sister's certainty and single-mindedness. The other is limited to a small circle consisting of parents, relatives, and two or three friends who set her standards in life—from food and house furnishings to politics, sex, religion, and recreation—and the moral universe seems to have the unity of the simple society of the past. It would appear that it is the working-class girl, rather than her middle-class sister, who leads the sheltered life.

For the happiest third of blue-collar couples in my study, life contains many satisfactions. The birth of a child ("I get real set up when one of them gets born"); the downpayment on a house; a good carpentry job; an unexpected gift brought by the husband ("a real classy box of candy"); a good report card brought by a child; sexual satisfaction ("Sex is a big thing with us"); a family reunion of relatives; watching the children at play ("They are really comical"); a new bedroom set—these and other things are sources of pleasure. And for many, there is the satisfaction of feeling they are honorably fulfilling the roles of provider, mate, and parent.

But the moral certainties of the blue-collar world, for all their allure, do not insure happiness, and the fact is that by and large these working-class couples are less satisfied with marriage and less happy with life in general than the better-educated middle classes. The assessment of marital happiness is a precarious venture, but the indications are that marital happiness rises with the ascent from working-to middle-class status. Thus, at a time when nostalgia for moral simplicities appears particularly acute, my journey into the past has a certain relevance. If many of our social ills are the product of the moral confusion that has grown out of exposure to diverse ideas and changing circumstances, it does not follow that clear moral directives and consensus are synonomous with social health. Marriage roles may be clearly defined, yet unsatisfactory. The isolation that shields the blue-collar workers from some of the ills of modern life serves also to bar them from its benefits. It prevents the dissemination of values and ideas that would promote marital happiness under conditions of modern life. Whereas middle-class couples today regard companionship as one of the functions of marriage, those in the working class tend to differentiate sharply between the mental worlds of the sexes, and do not include friendship between the spouses in their model of marriage. Marriage without friendship may have been viable when married couples remained close to relatives and trusted friends, but these working class families do, after all, live in an industrial and changing society and are subject to many of its pressures; geographical mobility is increasing. A spokesmen for the Department of Labor was quoted in *The New York Times* (September 20, 1963) as saying: "Many more of our workers than in the past must have, or develop, the mobility to shift jobs. . . . Many may have to change their residence." Separated from kin and friends, married couples must increasingly turn to each other for emotional support and friendship.

A family I shall call the Robinsons illustrates some of the problems of these couples. Mr. and Mrs. Robinson, aged 25 and 23 respectively, are grammar school graduates, married three years, and the parents of two infants. Mr. Robinson earns about $4,000 a year.

Mr. Robinson leaves child care and housework completely to his wife and spends most of his leisure away from home with male friends. He and Mrs. Robinson accept this as normal. "If you do right by your job and by the woman [sexually], they owe you some rest to yourself." "The husband earns the money, don't he? He has the right to get away as often as he wants." Of friendship between the sexes, Mrs. Robinson says: "Regular guys don't mess around with women except when they want what a woman's got to give them. Men and women are different; men don't feel the same as us. The fellows got their interests and the girls got theirs, they each go their separate ways." Mr. Robinson asks, "What is it about women that they want to talk about things when there is really nothing to talk about? Why do they have to hash it over? They talk about screwy things. Keep quacking, like beating a dead horse."

Mrs. Robinson, though she accepts her husband's absences, feels lonely and trapped at home with her two infants. Her mother works, and Mrs. Robinson has no relatives or close friends in the neighborhood. She is irritable and depressed, and an atmosphere of gloom pervades the home. This perplexes Mr. Robinson—all the more so because their sexual relations are highly satisfactory to both. As he behaves in ways sanctioned by their circle, it never occurs to him that there may be some connection between his wife's irritability and his own behavior.

Mrs. Robinson's dissatisfaction with her life is great, but she is at a loss to explain it. Her husband's neglect of her appears quite normal, as does his occasional violence, and she never expected companionship in marriage. But accepting these circumstances does not alleviate her loneliness. Mr. and Mrs. Robinson's conception of marriage without friendship and their lack of mutual understanding combine to intensify their unhappiness. But being largely isolated from the intellectual mainstream of society, they are slow to modify their conceptions of marriage in ways that might help them to happiness.

What may we infer from the plight of the Robinsons and others in their circumstances? It seems fair to conclude from my study that the spread to the semiskilled and the less educated wage earners of the middle-class habits of consumption has not been accompanied by a similar spread of mental outlook and social behavior. From all appearances, the working-class style of life—its values, attitudes, institutions—remains in many respects quite distinct from the dominant middle-class patterns of contemporary American society. Life at its best is economically comfortable, but for the great majority it is narrowly circumscribed by the family, the relatives, a few friends, the union, the boss, the church. Nothing is visible in the vast darkness beyond this limited circle but a few movie stars, athletes, and some national office holders. Social life is limited to two or three couples, and many have no joint social life whatever, apart from visiting relatives. They do not read books. Television, radio, and the newspapers bring in something of the outside world, but past research has revealed how selective is the response to the mass media and how weak the impact when compared to the influence of close associates. Blue-collar families lack even such links with society as may be provided by membership in women's clubs or the Rotary. The labor union occasionally provides this sort of link for the men, but only infrequently. In short, these working men and their wives—English-speaking, well-dressed, and well-mannered— do not enjoy full membership in the American society.

We know from other studies that about one-third of the children of manual workers can be expected to rise to a higher stratum of society. But what of the remaining two thirds? Almost without exception, the fathers hope their sons will not become semiskilled workers; they want them to "go a lot further." Yet whatever their hopes, the milieu in which they live will be perpetuated for the majority of their children unless measures are taken to help them to a better life. The restricted environment and the low cultural level of the home hinder the development of their children from the first years of life on, retard the development of intellectual interests and motivation, and diminish the children's chances for higher education. The resources of the schools must be improved so that working-class children can be given from an early age the stimulation they lack at home; vocational counseling, a commonplace in the better schools, is sorely needed in the schools blue-collar children attend; and civic organizations must somehow make the effort to reach their parents. Until they do, there will remain a gap between the wage earners and the salaried middle classes, socially as well as materially; the working class will live on the fringe of society, and the antipoverty movement directed at the stratum below theirs will go only part way toward fulfilling the American promise.

6

Psychological Study of Whole Families

GERALD HANDEL

In his article "Abnormalities of Behavior," White (1959) introduces a group of references on schizophrenia with this comment: "It is reassuring to find that several workers are using the concept of interaction patterns in families rather than the questionable cause-effect model of parent influencing child [p. 279]." The implied rarity of this concept in the psychological literature is indicated by the fact that four of the five publications White mentions are of psychiatric origin, while only one is psychological; the rarity is underscored by the fact that Hoffman and Lippitt's (1960) entire presentation of family research methods in child psychology is cast explicitly within the cause–effect framework of parent influencing child.

There is an ambiguity in White's term "interaction patterns in families." On the one hand, it may be taken to mean

From *Psychological Bulletin*, Vol. 63, 1965, pp. 19–41. Copyright 1965 by the American Psychological Association.

interaction between some but not all members of a family, such as interaction between husband and wife (Tharp, 1963), mother and child, father and child, or child and child. Hoffman and Lippitt report that studies of parent–child interaction are increasing and they suggest that this is partly because of the failure of the simple parent–child cause–effect model.

White's term may, on the other hand, be taken to refer to interaction of all the family members, whether the whole family be defined as the nuclear or conjugal family whose members share a common household or the extended family residing in one or more households. The concept of family interaction in this broader sense has scarcely gained notice in psychology, although psychiatry (Group for the Advancement of Psychiatry, 1954), anthropology (Lewis, 1950, 1959, 1961), sociology (Hill, 1949; Parsons and Bales, 1955), and social work (Voiland, 1962) are giving it increasing attention. Psychology has been concerned with events within the family but has made little effort to conceptualize and study the family as a unit.

This paper reports the progress made thus far in studying whole families. Attention is given to work by investigators and thinkers in psychology and related fields. The paper does not deal with two-person interaction, partly because discussions of work in this area are already available (Eisenstein, 1956; Hoffman and Lippitt, 1960; Tharp, 1963), but mainly because moving beyond the two-person framework has proved to be an especially difficult problem. The discussion is not restricted, however, to interaction in the sense of studies of face-to-face behavior. The problem focus is the psychological study of the family as a whole, and observation of face-to-face interaction is only one of the procedures that have been used. If the parent–child, cause–effect model has been only slightly successful, there are grounds for believing that studies of two-person, parent–child interaction, which omit observation of other family members, will also prove of limited value for understanding child personality. But quite apart from evaluations of the merit of two-person interaction studies in child psychology, the psychological study of whole families is of interest in its own right.

The adequacy, though not the utility, of the interaction concept—regardless of whether the data be obtained by direct observation of face-to-face behavior or by subject reports—is itself problematic, even for the study of whole families. One of the many reasons the burgeoning field of small group study has scarcely concerned itself with the family is perhaps the recognition that the ahistoric framework appropriate for ad hoc laboratory groups is not well suited to the family, which is constituted by enduring interpersonal relationships. Strodtbeck (1954), in one of the few small-group studies using families as subjects, tested propositions derived from ad hoc groups and found important differences which he explained on the basis of these enduring relationships (pp. 28–29). Later work by Strodtbeck (1958) seems clearly to indicate that family interaction can only be understood in conjunction with the family's prevailing interpersonal relationships. The question may be put, then, whether interaction or interpersonal relationship will prove the more fruitful concept in understanding families or, indeed, whether adequate investigation will not require data on both kinds of phenomena as reciprocally determining. (To use both concepts interchangeably as though they were equivalent, as is sometimes done, can only lead to obscuring important problems.)

Thus far, we have been using the term whole family as a means of differentiating a field of study that lies beyond the traditional study of subfamily pairs such as the mother–child pair. For our purposes the term serves adequately, but notice must be taken that its referent is not precise. An issue centers on whether it is fruitful to select the nuclear family as a unit of study or whether adequate understanding requires study of the extended family. Some investigators (Handel and Hess, 1956; Hess and Handel, 1959) have argued that, regardless of the ties that link a nuclear family to kin and wider social groups, there is a sense in which the nuclear family is a bounded universe. The nuclear family is a meaningful unit of study because, typically, its members inhabit a common household which is not shared with relatives; within these boundaries—the home—the family members develop long-sustained, relatively more intense and meaningful relationships among each other than with outsiders, including kin residing in other households. Spiegel and Bell (1959), on philosophical and anthropological grounds, consider this viewpoint too narrow for understanding psychopathology. They consider it essential to view the nuclear family as a component of the extended family and the entire family network as embedded in a larger social and cultural network, if the emotional disturbance of a particular family member is to be adequately understood. The problem of defining the unit of study is discussed briefly by Leichter (1961) who concludes that "the family unit may shift according to the purpose of analysis [p. 143]."

In passing, it may be noted that Spiegel and Bell make common cause with White, Hoffman and Lippitt, Ackerman (1958), and others in questioning the adequacy of the cause-effect model of parent influencing child. Most of the work reviewed in this article has similar import. Some studies focus on the extended family (e.g., Cleveland and Longaker, 1957; Fisher and Mendell, 1956; Mendell and Fisher, 1956) while others focus on the nuclear family (e.g., Ackerman and Sobel, 1950; Frenkel-Brunswik, 1955; Hess and Handel, 1959).

EMERGENCE OF THE PROBLEM

Any discussion of the problem of conceptualizing and investigating whole families must begin with Burgess's (1926) formulation: "The Family as a Unity of Interacting Personalities."[1] From the perspective of contemporary psychology this is a remarkable phrase, as far reaching in its implications as it is compact in expression. It provides a basic orientation that can guide many research programs, regardless of how the unit of study be defined.

First, we may note that the formulation calls attention to the fact that a family is made up of persons, each with an individuality of his own, a personality. By implication, it seems to call in question the cause–effect model which locates independent variables exclusively in the parents and dependent variables exclusively in the children. At the very least, it suggests an alternative perspective in which each family member is regarded as a source of some relatively autonomous action. A child, as well as a parent, is construed as having individuality. Sufficient ground for this assumption is provided by the fact that each child in a family has a unique ordinal position. (The question of whether children in a particular ordinal position differ systematically from children in other ordinal positions is irrelevant here. The point is that within any given family, the first-, second-, and thirdborn, etc., can be expected to be different from each other in significant ways.) Other grounds for the assumption can be adduced, though one would also like to have studies of such dimensions as perceptual sensitivity and activity level of infants (Bergman and Escalona, 1949; Escalona and Heider, 1959; Escalona and Leitch, 1952; Fries and Woolf, 1954) conducted on infants in the same family. However, it is apposite to point out that one of the research problems immediately suggested by the Burgess (1926) formulation is the problem of how different children in the same family develop different identities. The problem is implicit in any effort to understand why one child develops a mental illness while other children in the same family do not. Uniqueness of ordinal position provides a basis for expecting that the personalities of children in the same family will differ from each other in some way, but what those differences will turn out to be and the processes by which they come about require research on whole families. One process is indicated in Harris' (1959) study, where he reports that: "Both the mothers and the fathers in our study invariably showed evidence of using their parenthood to continue or to resolve, through their children, some aspects of their own growing up, and therefore each of their several children might represent a somewhat different aspect of their past" [p. 39]. The same child can, of course, represent different things to the two parents.

By characterizing the family as a unity of interacting personalities, Burgess points to the problem of understanding interaction and interpersonal relationships in terms of the personalities
of the participating members. A recent attempt by Miller
(1961) to present an organized framework for dealing with the
problem is a valuable contribution and perhaps the most explicit statement yet available. It is, however, framed in terms of
two-person relationships, and modifications would undoubtedly
be required in order for it to be applicable to family groups.

It should be noted that the central research problem raised
by Burgess is not that of socialization, child training, or transmission of personality characteristics from parent to child but a
problem that is in a sense anterior to these, while also having
social psychological interest in its own right. The problem may
be phrased: *How do the several personalities in a family
cohere in an ongoing structure that is both sustained and
altered through interaction?* Regarded in this way, Burgess'
formulation may be seen as, in effect, a charter for the study of
whole families. As such, it demands research which (*a*) is
directed to conceptualizing the family as a unit; (*b*) studies the
personalities of the several members and the interrelationships
among them; (*c*) obtains data from each member of the
family. The Burgess formulation thus points to a unified psychological approach in which the intrapsychic processes and
personality structures of family members are considered in
conjunction with the interrelations among the members. This is
a tall order, and it cannot be said that the nature of such a
psychology is now at all clear. Nonetheless, some definite steps
in this direction have been taken, as this article hopes to
indicate. The problems are formidable, and the writings of
workers in this field often contain confessions of burdensome
difficulty. It seems clear that the application of widely accepted
concepts of methodological rigor in psychology must, in this
field, be adapted and perhaps deferred pending the development of both a minimally adequate conceptual framework and
hypotheses that seem fruitful enough to warrant rigorous test-

ing. Due recognition must be made of the recency of effort in this field. It is hoped that the survey presented here contributes a sufficient sharpening of focus to make possible a more concentrated and rigorous research.

Burgess's (1926) concept has received great veneration and reiteration in family sociology, but for about a quarter of a century little effort seems to have been made to pursue its implications. In his study of family adjustment to the stresses of war separation and reunion, Hill (1949) referred to thinking at the family level as third-dimensional in contradistinction to thinking at the level of the individual and the pair—one- and two-dimensional, respectively. He noted that third-dimensional thinking had only recently been attempted.

A beginning of psychoanalytic attention to the whole family is evident in the 1930s. The International Congress of Psychoanalysis in 1936 was devoted to the topic "The Family Neurosis and the Neurotic Family" (Grotjahn, 1959). Ackerman's (1938) first paper on family unity came soon after. Oberndorf (1938) and Mittelman (1944, 1948) broke with the orthodox psychoanalytic rule that the analyst should treat only one person in a family and avoid contact with the relatives; each was analyzing concurrently both partners to a marriage.

Psychiatric attention is now beginning to move from two-person relationships in the family to the whole family. Several considerations prompt this shift. One is that the disordered behavior of the patient is coming to be viewed as involving a certain stabilization of relationships with other family members so that the changes in the patient's behavior resulting from therapy disrupt these relationships, often with untoward consequences for other family members. Improvement in the patient is sometimes accompanied by the development of symptoms in other family members; the symptoms are transitive, but the therapeutic effects often are not (Jackson, 1957; Jackson and Weakland, 1959, 1961). However, Fisher and Mendell (1958) report instances of a spread of therapeutic effect from patient to family members not in therapy. One of the tasks of family study is to discover the conditions that favor the spread of symptoms and those that favor the spread of therapeutic effects.

Another consideration is that improved behavior in family relationships is seen as a criterion of therapeutic progress, but such progress cannot always be effected if other parties to the relationship are not engaged in the therapy. Ackerman (1956) states that he finds it increasingly difficult to carry therapy to successful completion without dealing directly with other family members so as to restore healthy family relationships (p. 140).

It is evident that in the thinking of Ackerman (1954) and others the concepts of mental health and illness are changing. These workers view the family, and not the individual, as the primary locus of mental health or illness. Bowen (1960), reporting research on a treatment program in which the families of schizophrenic patients lived with the patients in the hospital, states his view that "The schizophrenic psychosis of the patient is, in my opinion, a symptom manifestation of an active process that involves the entire family [p. 346]." Similar views are found in the work of Jackson and his colleagues and Lidz and his colleagues, which will be discussed below.

These newer psychiatric concepts have led to various innovations in therapy. The newer techniques include: (a) outpatient treatment of the whole family as a group by one therapist, which Jackson (1961) calls conjoint family therapy; (b) diagnostic evaluation of the whole family in order to select one member as the most suitable candidate for therapy in order to induce change in the whole family; (c) residence of the immediate family of the schizophrenic patient in the hospital with him, with individual therapy of the patient and group therapy of the family proceeding concurrently; (d) family group counseling (Freeman, Klein, Riehman, Lukoff, and Heisey, 1963). In addition, concurrent but individual therapy of husband and wife or parent and child by two therapists who compare notes increases in prevalence. Although clinical reports of this work grow in frequency as therapists report their efforts to devise more effective therapies, no systematic evaluations are yet available, so far as this writer is aware. Discussions of the various family therapies and their rationales are presented by Ackerman (1958, 1961) and Grotjahn (1960). Grotjahn's book includes a historical overview of developing psychoanalytic interest in family therapy, while Ackerman's (1958) book contains a discussion of changing concepts of personality which underlie this trend.

CONCEPTUAL VANTAGE POINTS

In recent years, several workers have addressed themselves to the psychological problem raised by the Burgess (1926) formulation, the problem of family unity. They have approached it in several ways; a review of them will form the subject of this section. First, however, a conceptual and terminological clarification is necessary. The term family unity is not in vogue these days, having been replaced by several terms which distribute its meaning: family homeostasis (Jackson, 1957), equilibrium (Parsons and Bales, 1955), integration, and solidarity. All of these terms involve viewing the family as a system, and there is overlap among them, but the first two seem more appropriate for describing interaction and its short-range shifts, while the latter two seem more appropriate for describing interpersonal relations in their more enduring aspect. One further distinction needs to be made. Bossard and Boll (1950) state: "We use the term 'family integration' to mean the welding or unification of its diverse elements into a complex whole or harmonious relationship [p. 199]." It is evident that this definition commingles two elements which are not only analytically distinct but the relationships between which pose empirical problems. Harmonious relationships refer to feelings of well-being or absence of deep conflicts, whereas the welding of diverse elements into a complex whole carries no such connotation. In fact, the work on families of psychiatric patients reveals that such families are often tightly integrated in such a way as to preclude harmony. One of the tasks of psychological research on families can well be to discover which kinds of integration lead to harmony and feelings of well-being among the members and which do not. It is clearly useful to distinguish integration, a construct that can deal with family systems in a nonevaluative way, from harmony, a term that refers to a widely valued family goal. Instead of harmony, however, it seems better to adopt the term solidarity which, as defined by Cousins (1960), can be operational. Integration and solidarity refer to somewhat different aspects of family life; the relationships between them constitute a subject worthy of research. Further, studies can be designed to show how various kinds of interaction (such as, e.g., in conjoint family therapy) affect both integration and solidarity.

We consider now the various conceptual vantage points that have been used in studying whole families.

Family and Culture

Psychologists have become increasingly familiar with the anthropological concept of culture. The importance of the anthropological perspective in understanding personality development was dramatized by Margaret Mead's (1928) pioneering study of adolescence in Samoa and received increased recognition with the publication of Kluckhohn and Murray's (1948) collection of papers in personality and culture. Kaplan's (1961) recent collection indicates that this approach has developed greatly in sophistication.

Until recently, it has been customary to regard the culture or some particular general feature of it—notably the child-rearing practices typical in the culture—as an independent variable and personality as a directly dependent variable. Attention is beginning to shift—very slightly—toward consideration of the individual family as mediating agent of the culture. Cleveland and Longaker (1957) examined the impact of cultural factors on individual mental health by analyzing the transmission and mediation of values in a family setting. In a report deriving from the Stirling County study directed by Alexander Leighton, they studied one kinship group which contributed several patients to the caseload of a small-town clinic in Nova Scotia. On the basis of data derived from psychotherapy, psychological tests, and home visits with relatives, they conclude that the neurotic patterning found in the family is a function of two processes: (*a*) value conflict within the culture; (*b*) a culturally recurrent mode of self-disparagement, with roots in the child-rearing methods, linked to the failure of individuals to adjust to incompatible value orientations. The value clash was between a striving orientation, involving personal ambition, acceptance of a rational money economy, and emphasis on personal responsibility for success and failure, and, on the other hand, a traditional orientation, emphasizing physical labor in an outdoor setting, strong desires for personal independence and integrity, and currently meaningful activities as opposed to longer range goals. According to the authors' analysis, self-disparagement develops when: (*a*) the parents, oscillating between the conflicting value orientations, present contradictory models of behavior to their children; (*b*) the child develops one of the orientations which he has incorporated in his personality; (*c*) an obstacle to learning develops in a life area relevant to the already vulnerable and devalued personality segment. In terms of this process, they report a case in which a father, his son, and the father's first cousin developed neurotic behavior disorders.

From the standpoint developed in the present paper, the study just described is incomplete since it does not explore the reasons why other family members did not become neurotic. Presumably some family process is operating selectively. The study is useful, however, because it explicitly interposes the family, as an element of analysis, between the culture and the individual. It suggests the necessity of more microscopic studies of socialization, raising new questions. Instead of the broad question—How are children socialized in this culture?—it suggests that we must ask the more specific question of how a child is socialized into a particular family or—hopefully—type of family. Relevant to this point is a study under way directed by Spiegel and F. Kluckhohn, described by Spiegel and Bell

(1959) but not yet reported in detail. Their study closely parallels the Cleveland-Longaker study (1957) —the approach to value analysis used by both pairs of investigators was in fact developed by Kluckhohn (1950) —but Spiegel and Kluckhohn seem to be pushing their clinical analysis further than did Cleveland and Longaker.

Spiegel and Kluckhohn, though moving in a new direction by comparing families with and without an emotionally disturbed child in three subcultural groups, work with the prevailing framework that locates values in the culture (or ethnic and social class subculture). They then analyze family behavior as a response to these external standards. There are, however, signs of a more radical view which is stated by J. Henry (1951), an anthropologist interested in personality development and clinical problems: "every family is almost a different culture [p. 800]." Roberts (1951) studied three neighboring Navaho households and judged that they constituted discrete local cultures, though interlocking. Bott (1957), in her study of family roles and norms in London, states that she started out with the idea of first determining cultural definitions of family roles and then seeing how the members' personalities governed their role performances. But she found so much variation not only in role performance but the role definition, because the environment permits wide latitude of choice, that she was obliged to adopt a more psychological and family-centered view.

These anthropologists thus espouse the view that each family, as a small group, develops its own norms, values, and role definitions. The general case for such a viewpoint has been familiar to psychologists since the early work of Sherif (1936), but its application to families is relatively recent. It is not a widely disseminated view among anthropologists, nor has it received much attention in social psychology as practiced by both psychologists and sociologists, although Frenkel-Brunswik (1955) adopted and exemplified it in her comparison of the social outlooks of an authoritarian and an equalitarian family. Whether it is useful to consider each individual family as having a culture of its own in any strict sense is open to question. But the effort to do so is nonetheless worthwhile in sensitizing us to the fact that analyses of values and norms that are useful at a macrosocial level need refinement when applied at the microsocial level. In the series of midwestern American families reported by Hess and Handel (1959) and Handel (1962), there are four upper-middle-class families all of whom can be regarded as manifesting the striving orientation defined by Kluckhohn. This orientation takes different forms in the four families: one emphasizes responsibility; one, independence; one, competition; and one reveals marked conflict between independence and responsibility. It is useful to consider them as similar when comparing them with families from a nonstriving society, but these four families have different consequences for the personalities of their respective component members.

Family Interaction, Interpersonal Relationships, and Personality

Burgess, in the article referred to, says that he was tempted to call the family a superpersonality. Although this term has since been carefully avoided, some of the work devoted to the study of whole families in fact involves an attempt to characterize them in personality terms. These characterizations are arrived at either through an analysis of family interaction or through an analysis of the personalities of the several family members or through a combination of these approaches. The idea that groups, including families, each have a distinctive psychological character is implicit in earlier work. Lewin, Lippitt, and White's (1939) concept of social climate is an important forerunner. Their categorization of groups as authoritarian, democratic, and laissez-faire has found its way into discussions of the effects of the family on children's behavior. In the latter context, however, these categories are categories of parent behavior rather than of families.

Recent work frequently shows several features which differentiate it from previous practice: (*a*) Instead of using predetermined categories such as authoritarian and democratic, no assumption is made in advance as to which dimensions are likely to prove most significant for a particular family. A meaningful system or set of family categories is seen as lying in the future, present efforts being exploratory steps toward that goal. Although the importance of categories referring to how power is exercised in the family is indisputable, the familiar dimensions such as power and warmth quite obviously do not exhaust the range of significant family phenomena, and to focus on the effects of these dimensions at the expense of searching out and formulating others can only result in premature closure. (*b*) Instead of using the cause-effect model of parent influencing child, the family is conceptualized as a group. (*c*) The personalities of the component members and/or the interplay between intrapsychic and group processes constitute the data matrix from which the concepts are built. This conceptual procedure does not usually take the route of analyzing the personality of each family member in detail before proceeding to the group characterization. Rather, personality materials are examined in order to move directly to characterization of group processes. Family interaction is thus conceived as occurring at the personality level.

A pioneering study exemplifying this viewpoint is that of J. Henry (1951) who proposed that a neurosis can be considered a rigid intrafamilial interaction pattern that is pathogenic in quality. The transmission of the neurosis in the family is the transmission of this pathogenic interaction pattern. Henry studied records of a psychiatric social worker's interviews with the mother of a boy referred to a child guidance clinic. He recognized the limitations imposed by using data obtained only from one member of the family, but at the time of his study these were the best data available for the task he set himself. Using ad hoc categories, he coded every intrafamilial interaction reported by the mother in interviews extending over a period of about 2 years, including interactions between the mother and her own mother and brother, as well as within the nuclear family. The coding procedure enabled him to summarize the interaction pattern of each pair and triad of family members. On the basis of this analysis of family interaction episodes reported by the patient's mother, Henry diagnosed the family as one in which tendencies to dominance, provocation, and clinging are worked out. This family is contrasted with one reported earlier the same year by Henry and Warson (1951) and diagnosed as narcissistic. Henry makes an observation that is important in any attempt to conceptualize families in psychological terms. He points out that family traits are scattered unevenly among family members and may not occur at all in some members. Each family member may embody the pathology in a different way, and some may be free from it. This scatter phenomenon is found repeatedly in the studies reported in this paper and it can safely be assumed that all families will manifest psychologically significant intermember diversity. If there is to be any successful psychological classification of families, it cannot rest upon any simple search for personality similarity among members but will have to be founded upon some conception of dynamic interplay among members, a conclusion which is clearly implied also by Hoffman and Lippitt (1960).

Interaction is a diffuse concept, as yet insufficiently analyzed. It is used to refer to a variety of phenomena which may be regarded as not yet codified components or levels of interaction. Among these are: *physical contacts* such as those of mothering; *cognitive interchanges* in which information is exchanged and which proceed toward a definition of reality (as in Sherif's autokinetic experiments) or toward decision making (as in Bales's interaction-process analysis); behavior in which *norms* and *roles* are created and validated, or in which *selves* are discovered and created (predominantly a sociological usage but also exemplified in such diverse psychological writers as Piaget, Rogers, and Sullivan); *affective behavior,* in which feelings and emotions are transmitted or exchanged (as in much psychiatric writing, perhaps most explicitly in that of Sullivan). There are various concepts of interaction which cross-cut or are at a higher level of abstraction than the categories just named, such as G. H. Mead's theory of symbolic interaction (Rose, 1962) or other theories of communication, of which that advanced by Bateson, Jackson, and their colleagues will be discussed below.

Although in no way attempting to codify interaction phenomena, Hess and Handel (1959) offered some rudiments of a framework for analyzing family interaction and interpersonal relationships, a framework which is psychologically relevant, which seems capable of fruitful development, and which is capable of encompassing a number of other studies already published. On the basis of their study of nonclinical midwestern American families, they advanced a number of concepts which simultaneously refer to the personalities of the individual family members and the character of the family as a group. First, they postulate that *separateness and connectedness are the underlying conditions of a family's life* and that *a basic family process is the effort to achieve a satisfactory pattern of separateness and connectedness.* As each member of a family develops his own personality, adapts to changes through the life cycle, seeks gratification and, generally, creates an individual life space, he also is involved in more or less binding ties with other family members, ties which he endeavors to create and ties which the other members endeavor to create with him. These ties are likewise expressions of the several personalities involved, as well as of many other kinds of factors.

In the course of establishing patterns of separateness and connectedness each member of a family develops an image of each other member. That is, each family member comes to invest each other member with particular cognitive and affective meaning and significance. These images have certain stable aspects but they also change as the family members move through the life cycle. A second process which these authors identify is that *behavior in a family may be viewed as the family's effort to attain a satisfactory congruence of images through the exchange of suitable testimony.* This family interaction comes to be centered around a particular theme in each family. Themes found in the families reported include: flight from insecurity, equanimity and its vicissitudes, dynamics of disconnectedness, demonstration of constructive independence, and comforts and crises of companionship. A family's theme does not, of course, find identical expression in the personalities of each member; this is implied by the two processes previously described. The theme describes the centering of the family's interaction. Although the concept of theme was developed from qualitative data, the concept has a logical foundation analogous to concepts of central tendency used for quantitative data. By implication and further analogy, therefore, a family's interaction may be considered to have a dispersion. Eventually, it may be possible to compare families both qualitatively and quantitatively in terms of dispersion as well as the centering of their interactions.

Hess and Handel (1959) indentify another family process which is, in a sense, a qualitative formulation of dispersion: *establishing boundaries of the family's world of experience.* As each family maps its domain of acceptable and desirable experience it raises signposts for goals and signals for danger. But these boundaries, which lie within persons as well as among them, are continually tested as new experiences occur, new feelings arise, and new actions are taken. Limits to experience are established in a veriety of ways and along several dimensions. Four particularly important dimensions are: the differentiation of individual personality, the intensity of experience, the extensity of experience, and the tendency to evaluate experience.

The last process which these writers identify is: *dealing with significant given biosocial issues of family life,* particularly sex, generation, and birth order. These issues include not only sexuality and authority but, more broadly, how each generation and each sex is defined in terms of feelings, rewards, and restraints.

Interaction gives rise to interpersonal relationships within the family. These relationships do not merely follow the intrinsic lines of sex and age but derive from the interlocking meanings which the members have for one another. Hess and Handel propose the term pattern of alignment to refer to the distribution of ties among members of a family. This concept is broader than that of coalition as it is used in small-group research. Whereas coalition refers to the phenomenon of teaming up to exercise power, pattern of alignment includes any basis on which family members line up with each other, unconsciously as well as consciously, in fantasy as well as in action, for reasons of comfort or affection as well as those of power, to enhance each other as well as to defeat each other. From a psychological point of view, the intrapsychic bases of affiliation are as important as the fact of it, both for the persons affiliating and for the group as a whole. Redl's (1942) study of group emotion in school classrooms has useful implications for the study of families. Clearly the phenomena included under pattern of alignment require differentiation and codification just as do those subsumed under interaction. Just as clearly, the concept points to needed areas of research. To name but one, we require research on sibling support (including identification of siblings with one another) that will balance our research into sibling rivalry. It is not unreasonable to suppose that the relative primacy of sibling support as against sibling rivalry is a factor affecting mental health, and personality formation generally. But sibling relationships are part of the total pattern of alignment in a family and they will be adequately understood only if studied in that context. It is evident from everything that has been said thus far in this paper that the personalities of the parents and the motives and meanings they bring to bear in their interaction with their children contribute to the kind of sibling relationships their children will develop.

Hess and Handel (1959) developed their concepts in the course of studying nonclinical families. Several reports of clinical research suggest that these concepts are potentially fruitful for understanding behavior disturbances of various kinds. Distortions in the separateness-connectedness pattern are seen as contributing to clinical behavior pathology. Wynne, Ryckoff, Day, and Hirsch (1958) take as their basic assumption that every human being strives both to form relationships with others and to develop a sense of personal identity. They conceive that the effort to solve this dual problem leads to two main kinds of solutions, mutuality and pseudomutuality. (They also recognize a third category, nonmutual complementarity, which is not relevant in the present context.) Mutuality entails recognition and appreciation of divergence of self-interests. Pseudomutuality is characterized by preoccupation with fitting together at the expense of the identities of the people in the relationship. Drawing on their work with families of late adolescents and young adults who have suffered acute schizophrenia, the authors develop the hypothesis that the relationships in these families that are acceptable and may be openly acknowledged are intensely and enduringly pseudomutual. Although they do not claim either that pseudomutuality in itself produces schizophrenia or that it is unique to the relations of schizophrenics, they do find that it is a significant feature of the setting in which reactive schizophrenia develops. Pseudomutuality is sustained by various mechanisms all of which make it difficult for the potential schizophrenic to differentiate himself as an individual with his own identity. Following Parsons and Bales, the authors propose that the potential schizophrenic internalizes the system of family relationships that keeps him from differentiating himself and that he thereby collaborates in maintaining the family pattern in which he is caught. Pseudomutuality requires concealment at the expense of openness, so that communication is distorted and perception blurred. A further result is that the roles enacted by the family members vis-à-vis each other are dissociated from subjective experience.

Pseudomutuality is a pathologically exaggerated form of connectedness which is established at the cost of the schizophrenic's failure to achieve a distinctive identity (Ryckoff, Day, and Wynne, 1959). Vogel and Bell (1960) described a pathological form of separateness in which a child is pushed into the role of family scapegoat and becomes emotionally disturbed (diagnosis unspecified). Their paper is an interim report from the Spiegel-Kluckhohn study described earlier. On the basis of intensive data from nine families—three Irish-American, three Italian-American, and three old American, all working class—they concluded that a characteristic pattern of events leads to emotional disturbance in a child. The elements of the pattern are as follows: (a) Between the parents major unresolved tensions exist, based on deep fears about their marital relationship. (b) The tensions are so severe that some discharge is necessary, but for various reasons the parents dare not seek a scapegoat outside the family. The powerlessness of the children invites selection of one of them as a scapegoat. (c) One particular child in the sibship most readily symbolizes the variety of social and psychological problems impinging on the family. He is "selected" as the scapegoat, and his subsequent behavior provides suitable testimony to the appropriateness of the initial selection. Selection of the particular child is governed by such factors as his sex, position in the birth order, intelligence, physical characteristics, and other factors which have a particular emotional meaning to the parents. The other children remain free of emotional disturbance. (d) The child is inducted into and sustained in the scapegoat role by the application of inconsistent parental expectations. Behavior which is explicitly criticized is implicitly encouraged. Or behavior discouraged by one parent is encouraged by the other. Or the parental expectations are inconsistent in their severity. (e) The scapegoat role is further sustained by several mechanisms. These include parental denial that the child is emotionally disturbed and parental definition of themselves as victims rather than the child. Further, preoccupation with the child serves the function of enabling the parents to avoid directly confronting their own problems.

Vogel and Bell's (1960) paper is an important one. If their analysis of the scapegoat process be regarded as a particular instance of a general process, we are provided with a new avenue to understanding personality formation. Their model

invites us to look at the ways in which the child's own characteristics and behavior are processed in the family by having
meanings attached to them by others, meanings which the child
variously resists, modifies, or cooperates in sustaining. In the
process of growing up, the child endeavors to create new
meanings for himself which the other family members are more
or less willing to share with him. His perceptual, cognitive,
affective, and motivational capacities and propensities mesh
with or collide with the corresponding capacities and propensities of the other members in such a way that the child is
encouraged or induced to grow into the particular kind of
person he is to become. Murphy's (1962) concept of coping is
relevant in this context because from birth the child is faced
with the task of coping with the meanings which his parents
and sibs impute to him and his behavior, while he works at
imputing meanings to them and their behavior. Vogel and Bell
do not present as full a description as we would like of how the
scapegoat copes with the meanings his parents assign to him,
but Wynne and his collaborators present some vivid examples
of how the young schizophrenic resists the meanings assigned
by the members of his family. Lidz, Fleck, Cornelison, and
Terry (1958) illustrate how the parental personalities influence
the meanings they assign to the behavior of children who
become schizophrenic.

Wynne (1961), following Hess and Handel (1959),
adopted the concept of alignment pattern in his study of schizophrenics. One of his main findings is that, in the families of
schizophrenics, alignments are highly unstable; this finding is at
variance with that reported by Bowen (1960). Neither writer
reports sufficient data to enable the reader to discern what
might account for the difference. Another finding by Wynne
indicates a situation in families of schizophrenics which seems
to be rather different from that in the families studied by
Vogel and Bell. He found it a great oversimplification to
consider the schizophrenic child a victim of schizophrenogenic
parents. Rather, all family members are engaged in reciprocally victimizing—and rescuing—processes. The difference be-

tween this conclusion and that of Vogel and Bell may be more
apparent than real, for the tension between the parents that
they discuss suggests that the scapegoat child is not the only
victim in the families they studied. Further, Vogel and Bell's
analysis reveals the reciprocating effects which the scapegoat
child has upon his parents, effects which sustain their own
personality and marital difficulties.

Cumulatively, the foregoing discussion strongly suggests that
the processes of personality formation and the processes of family integration are, to an important extent, the same phenomena.
While Parsons has made the point that personality, culture,
and social system are three different conceptualizations of the
same basic data, the point being made here is that when the
family is the focus of study it is necessary and possible for
some purposes to have a unified conceptualization which en-
compasses both the individual and the group. As the child
copes with the meanings attributed to his behavior by the other
family members, he both shapes his own personality and contributes to defining the pattern of separateness and connectedness in the family. The meanings assigned set limits, perhaps,
to the coping behavior he will be able to attempt, and in the
course of accepting, modifying, or resisting these limits the
child both works toward his own identity and builds particular
kinds of ties to other members. His ways of coping are at the
same time an important part of his contribution to his ties to
other members. The child's perceptual and cognitive adjustments, his cathexes, identifications, fantasies, acting out, and
all other emotional and behavioral manifestations are at one
and the same time constitutive of his own personality, constitutive of his ties to other members in a proactive sense (to use
Murray's term), and constitutive of the meaning he has as an
object for the other members.

Analysis of interpersonal relationships in the family is bound
to raise questions about the usefulness of the concept of role.
This is a vast topic in itself, and space limitations preclude an
adequate discussion. Suffice it to say in the present context
that, if the concept is to prove useful for psychological study of

families, we require more highly refined analyses than are yet available. Categories such as male and female roles or parent and child roles are, though necessary as a starting point, simply too gross for adequate understanding. One dimension of the problem is suggested by the Vogel and Bell study. The emotionally disturbed child may be said to occupy a scapegoat role. But do all emotionally disturbed children have comparable roles in their families? If so, how are we to distinguish in role terms between different kinds of emotionally disturbed children, or do these differences have nothing to do with role? An answer to this question does not seem to be available at the present time. Also, since a role is fully understandable only as part of a role system, we need to know what parental and sibling roles complete the system of what the scapegoat (or other roles of emotionally disturbed children) is a part. Further, we have yet to develop an adequate analysis of the various kinds of family roles of normal children—and, for that matter, of mother-wives and husband-fathers. Much greater efforts has been made to codify the phenomena of role (see, e.g., Goffman, 1961; Neiman and Hughes, 1951; Sarbin, 1954; Sargent, 1951) than the phenomena of interaction, but much remains to be done. Ackerman (1951, 1958) presents some ideas about role that are particularly useful for psychology, but neither he nor anyone else has yet given us systematic studies of whole families, making use of these ideas.

Fleck, Lidz, Cornelison, Schafer, and Terry (1959) and Fleck (1960) report that incestuous and homosexual themes are quite pronounced in the families of schizophrenic patients that they studied. The patient's intrapsychic conflicts over these kinds of sexual impulses reflect flagrantly seductive behavior by the parents.

The concept of family theme seems a useful one for a number of reasons. It provides a way of briefly summarizing the central psychological processes in a family group. Perhaps even more important, it is a stimulus to, and an avenue for, breaking out of the constraint of seeing families only in terms of power (authoritarian-democratic; dominant-submissive) and affection (strict–permissive; warm–cold). Power and affection as concepts constitute entirely too narrow a base for comprehending the rich psychological diversity of family life. Searching for themes prompts the investigator to gather a richer variety of data and to be more open to what the data reveal. At the same time, it must be recognized that the search for themes entails the potential (but as yet undemonstrated) disadvantage of endlessly idiosyncratic findings. Consequently, while some such summarizing concept seems useful for many purposes, it also appears necessary to develop some basis on which families may be systematically compared. A solution to this problem proposed by Handel (1962) and influenced by Kluckholn's mode-of-value analysis involves moving down one level of abstraction to focus on certain core dimensions which may be regarded as constituent elements of themes. Analyzing individually obtained TATs from each member of five four-person families, Handel found that the family themes obtained could be dissected to yield five orientation categories, so-called because they refer to the family's orientation or stance to the world. These were: nature of the external world, nature of the self, the source of goals, nature of action, and nature of heterosexuality. This list is not considered exhaustive.

Another important attempt to characterize whole families grows out of a social work context and is reported by Voiland (1962); the project began in St. Paul and was later extended to six other cities. A survey of social agency services in St. Paul showed that there was a small group of multiproblem families that made unusually heavy demands on the resources of many agencies. Initially, these disturbed families were classified in terms of marital axes—interaction patterns of the marital partners. Efforts to correlate other family problems with these axes were not successful.

The study then moved to a broader framework utilizing four main dimensions: (a) types of disorder in the family, including personality disorders of any member, financial disorders such as irregular income production, and family dissolution disorders due to desertion, divorce, separation, placement of children; (*b*) family social functioning, including marital, child rearing, child development, and financial; (*c*) individual characteristics of each member—personality, intellectual, and physical; (*d*) development of each parent in his family of origin.

On the basis of this framework, four types of disordered family were identified: perfectionistic, inadequate, egocentric, and unsocial. The types are presented as being supported by statistical analysis of systematically coded case data. These data are not presented in the book but are said to be available from the organization which sponsored the research.

Each family type is characterized by its own syndrome of disorders. For example, the perfectionistic family tends to involve parental concern about habit-training practices and concern about guiding self-reliance in the child; anxiety and guilt-ridden behavior in the child; problems of emotional give and take between the spouses and problems of maintaining mutual self-esteem; anxiety-dominated behavior patterns in one or both parents. These disorders are described as distorting realistic handling of problems without interfering with good social conduct. In contrast, the unsocial family's disorders tend to be child neglect and fostering of disrespect for social authority; delinquency, truancy, psychosis, or other serious personality disturbances of the child; multiple symptoms and rapidly changing attitudes in the marital relationship which often bring the parents into court or evoke complaints to police; divorce often followed by remarriage of the partners to each other; hospitalization for mental illness; crime; addictions; sexual deviations common in adult members.

Although the framework for analysis is heterogeneous, this study is notable in two respects. First, it is the only study known to the writer which attempts a psychosocial typology of whole families oriented to total family functioning rather than to some specific life area. Secondly, the study explicitly rejects interaction as a basis for family classification in favor of inter-personal relationships as the basis. . . .

RESEARCH METHODS

There are as yet no established methods for studying whole families. Nonetheless it is worthwhile calling attention, however briefly, to some of the most common procedures and some issues that are raised. The discussion can be no more than suggestive.

Therapy

Psychiatrists have increasingly been using family therapy as a research method. Various clinical research teams are filming and tape recording family therapy sessions and analyzing these in a search for significant relationships. As noted earlier, there are also attempts to study whole families on an in-patient basis (Bowen, 1960). In terms of volume, family therapy is probably the largest single source of data for whole family study at the present time. Should this situation continue, the psychological study of whole families may well repeat the history of personality study; conceptions of abnormal functioning will be dominant for a long time until, belatedly, studies of nonclinical families will be undertaken in an effort to achieve a more rounded view of how families function. The value of obtaining data from family therapy not only to develop more effective therapies but also to increase general understanding of the psychosocial dynamics of family life is not in dispute. The issue is whether studies of families in therapy should be the major source of knowledge in this field, to the relative neglect of other kinds of research. There can be little doubt that psychiatry now leads the way (although admittedly sometimes in collaboration with psychologists and other social scientists) in attempting to understand the family from a psychosocial point of view. If psychology as a discipline does not soon address itself more vigorously to this problem, the result may be that a generation hence psychologists will be devoting their time to trying to verify propositions originating in family psychiatry, just as in the field of personality study they have been significantly preoccupied with the merits of propositions originating in psychoanalysis.

Field Methods

As here used, this is an omnibus term which includes any procedure for obtaining data in the home of the subjects. Thus, interviewing, psychological testing, and observation of family interaction are field methods which have been used. These are, to be sure, diverse procedures, but the point of grouping them under this rubric is to call attention to the fact that the task of studying whole families that are normal or nonclinical poses a challenge for psychology, accustomed to dealing with easily accessible subjects in laboratories, clinics, nursery schools, and other captive or controlled environments. Useful discussions of some fieldwork problems and procedures in studies of whole nonclinical families will be found in Robb (1953), Bott (1957), and Hess and Handel (1959).

Projective Methods

Rosenzweig appears to have been the first psychologist to propose that close relatives of psychiatric patients, as well as the patients themselves, be given projective tests so that the diagnostician can understand the full psychodynamic setting of the patient's life (see Rosenzweig and Cass, 1954; Rosenzweig and Isham, 1947). Although projective techniques have been used before and since for the purpose of studying personality similarities, Rosenzweig and Isham's proposal is the first recognition that these techniques, particularly the TAT, can provide an avenue to understanding the psychic life of the family as a functioning unit. As noted earlier, Fisher and Mendell also used projective techniques in studying whole families, as did Hess and Handel.

Sohler, Holzberg, Fleck, Cornelison, Kay, and Lidz (1957) attempted to predict family interaction from analysis of a battery of projective tests, which included the TAT, Rorschach, Draw-A-Person, and Rotter Sentence Completion, individually administered to each member of a four-person family in which the son was hospitalized for schizophrenia. Over a 2-year period, the patient had been seen for 3 or 4 therapeutic hours per week; both his parents had been seen once a week; and his sister had been interviewed 29 times. All of this psychiatric-interview material constituted the criterion against which the psychological test interpretations were judged. The psychological report was dissected into 333 discrete interpretive statements about each family member and about family interaction. Although, overall, two thirds of these statements were found to agree with the psychiatric material, the individual personality descriptions contained the highest proportion of agreements, while predictions of attitude of one family member toward another and statements about family interaction were the most likely source of disagreements. Even so, some measure of success in this area is reported. Considering the novelty of the attempt, the results seem encouraging.

The interpretive approaches used by Rosenzweig and his associates. Fisher and Mendell, and Sohler et al., entail certain limitations which seem neither necessary nor desirable. First, all of these workers conceive of the family as a group of interrelated individuals but they do not also conceive of the family as having psychological properties of its own that are not explicitly attached to a specific member or pair of members. This restriction means that interpretations about family behavior are always from one person to another (e.g., how patient and mother relate to each other) and never from person to group or group to person. This latter type of conceptualization would seem to be necessary if, for example, one hoped to be able to use TAT data to make a diagnosis such as family scapegoat. Assessments of this order require thinking in group dynamic terms and not simply from person to person in point-to-point fashion, however necessary this way of thinking also is. In addition, of course, conceptualizing at the group level is also necessary if one wishes to use projective data to diagnose families in such terms as Voiland uses or Handel's orientation categories. Conceivably, although this remains to be determined, one might discover from the protocols obtained individually from each family member the family's communication rules as delineated by Haley—or other kinds of rules that might be thought of such as affective rules, defensive rules, rules for dealing with esteem-lowering events, etc.

A second limitation, found in the work of Fisher and Mendell, is the emphasis on responses which are unusual and yet are also similar among members, as in the example cited earlier. Focusing only on highly similar responses among family members leads one to ignore useful, perhaps necessary, data. Further, striking similarities of response among members are not always to be found; neither are highly unusual responses. It is necessary to have a procedure that is free of such limitations.

Handel (1962) proposed a method of TAT analysis for family study, called analysis of correlative meaning, which is not dependent upon the occurrence either of unusual responses or of similarity of members' responses, and which also makes possible analysis of psychological characteristics of a family as a group. The method, which makes use of W. E. Henry's (1951) horizontal-thematic analysis, rests upon three interlocking assumptions: (*a*) Each card of the TAT has a latent stimulus demand which is "the emotional problem or focus most generally raised by the picture. . . . It will vary from group to group somewhat" [W. E. Henry, 1956, p. 100]. (*b*) The meaning of any individual's stories is not exhausted by reference to his own personality; on the contrary, a part of the meaning of any individual's stories is discovered by reference to the stories of the other family members. (*c*) Family interaction gives rise to certain general problems and outlooks which involve each family member, each individual's response to a

TAT picture in part derives from his interaction with the other family members around the issues tapped by the picture, and the correlativity of meanings of the members' individually told stories derives from the prolonged interrelations of their experiences.[2] The orientation categories mentioned earlier were obtained by use of this method of interpretation. Its validity remains to be established, but the assumptions underlying it seem reasonable working assumptions.

Hess and Handel attempted a procedure in which a family as a group told stories to a set of specially designed, TAT-type pictures, an idea borrowed from W. E. Henry and Guetzkow (1951) who had successfully used this technique with nonfamily groups. In addition, the interaction of the families as they made up the joint stories was recorded with the aim of relating the overt interaction to the story material. Although some of this material is cited illustratively in Hess and Handel (1959), the technical and interpretive problems of relating the two kinds of data were not solved by the time their project was concluded. The potentiality of this method remains undetermined.

Controlled Experiment

Few controlled experiments using family groups are known to the writer. Certainly one of the few adequately reported ones, and perhaps the first, is that of Strodtbeck (1954). A unique aspect of this experiment is that it was carried out in the homes of the families rather than in a laboratory. Employing as subjects family groups consisting of father, mother, and adolescent son, Strodtbeck devised a procedure termed the revealed difference technique. Each family member was individually presented a list of 47 described situations and for each situation was asked to pick one of two alternatives. One such situation, for example, described two fathers discussing their sons: one a brilliant student and the other an outstanding athlete. The respondent was asked to decide which father was the more fortunate. After each family member had made his

47 choices, the investigator selected three items on which mother and father took one alternative and the son the other; three items on which mother and son had agreed but not the father; and three items on which father and son had agreed but not the mother. The family was then set to discussing these nine issues and urged to reach an agreement on each one. Their discussion was recorded and subsequently scored using the categories of Bales' interaction-process analysis. The interaction data were then analyzed in terms of the relationship between amount of activity in the discussion and number of decisions won. The experiment provides material for another form of analysis not pursued, namely, the symbolic meanings of agreement between each pair of members on different types of item. What, for example, is the difference between a family in which the mother and father but not the son agree that the father with the athletic son is the more fortunate and a family in which one parent and the son but not the other parent agree on this? Do we have any sound reason for believing that this type of analysis would be less illuminating than the interaction-process analysis? What is revealed by revealed differences? Would not the two types of analysis together be more informative than either alone?

Haley (1962) makes a strong plea for experiments with families and discusses some of the special problems involved in experimenting upon groups whose members have a long history of relationship. He argues that the goal of family experiments must be different from the goal of experimenting with ad hoc groups. Whereas the aim of experiments in social psychology is usually to demonstrate the effect of a particular set of conditions upon group performance, the goal of family experiments, as she sees it, is to describe and measure the way family members typically respond to each other, that is, outside the experimental situation. Although experiments with families do present certain difficulties, many discussed by Haley, it is questionable whether the logic underlying such experiments differs from the logic underlying other types of group experiment as radically as Haley believes it does. In this same paper he reports two experiments in which, all told, 30 families with

a schizophrenic member were compared with 30 normal
families. The experiments showed the families with a schizophrenic member had a harder time forming coalitions within
the family than did normal families. However, he himself
questions whether the results can be taken as demonstrating
the typical behavior of these families outside the experimental
situation. He suggests, however, that this latter problem can be
solved by running the same families several times in the same
experiment and by running them through different types of
experiment designed to test the same basic processes. More
generally, Haley sees experimentation as the procedure that
will yield a suitable classification of families, and he suggests
that whereas the first half of this century has been largely
devoted to classifying and describing individuals, the second
half of the century will likely be devoted to classifying families
and other ongoing organizations. Needless to say, he, like every
worker studying whole families, does not underestimate the
magnitude of the task, but neither does he overestimate its
importance.

NOTES

1. Most of the studies cited in this paper descend from the seminal thinking
of Freud, G. H. Mead, Cooley, and others. Since a full genealogy of
ideas is not attempted here, Burgess's formulation is the most appropriate
starting point. Further, no effort is made to show the relevance of the
work of such significant investigators as Lewin, Sullivan, Erikson, and
others; attention is restricted to writers who addressed themselves fairly
explicitly to the study of whole families.
2. I thank William E. Henry for suggestions which improved upon my initial
concatenation of these assumptions. If the linkage remains unclear, or is
proved untenable, the responsibility is mine alone. I express also my
appreciation to Sidney J. Levy and Lee Rainwater for their lively and helpful
interest in my efforts to use these assumptions in the interpretation of
data.

REFERENCES

Ackerman, N. W. The unity of the family. *Archives of Pediatrics*, 1938, 55,
51–62.
Ackerman, N. W. Social role and total personality. *American Journal of
Orthopsychiatry*, 1951, *21*, 1–17.

Ackerman, N. W. Interpersonal disturbances in the family: Some unsolved problems in psychotherapy. *Psychiatry,* 1954, *17,* 359–368.

Ackerman, N. W. Interlocking pathology in family relationships. In S. Rado and G. E. Daniels (Eds.), *Changing conceptions of psychoanalytic medicine.* New York: Grune and Stratton, 1956. Pp. 135–150.

Ackerman, N. W. *The psychodynamics of family life.* New York: Basic Books, 1958.

Ackerman, N. W. Emergence of family psychotherapy on the present scene. In M. I. Stein (Ed.), *Contemporary psychotherapies.* New York: Free Press of Glencoe, 1961. Pp. 228–244.

Ackerman, N. W., and Sobel, R. Family diagnosis: An approach to the pre-school child. *American Journal of Orthopsychiatry,* 1950, *20,* 744–753.

Bateson, G., Jackson, D. D., Haley, J., and Weakland, J. Toward a theory of schizophrenia. *Behavioral Science,* 1956, *1,* 251–264.

Bell, N. W. Extended family relations of disturbed and well families. *Family Process,* 1962, *1,* 175–193.

Bergman, P., and Escalona, Sibylle. Unusual sensitivities in very young children. *Psychoanalytic Study of the Child,* 1949, 4, 33–352.

Bossard, J. H. S., and Boll, Eleanor. *Ritual in family living.* Philadelphia: Univer. Pennsylvania Press, 1950.

Bott, Elizabeth. *Family and social network: Roles, norms and external relationships in ordinary urban families.* London: Tavistock, 1957.

Bowen, M. A family concept of schizophrenia. In D. D. Jackson (Ed.), *The etiology of schizophrenia.* New York: Basic Books, 1960. Pp. 346–372.

Burgess, E. W. The family as a unity of interacting personalities. *Family,* 1926, 7, 3–9.

Clausen, J. A., and Kohn, M. L. Social relations and schizophrenia: A research report and a perspective. In D. D. Jackson (Ed.), *The etiology of schizophrenia.* New York: Basic Books, 1960. Pp. 295–320.

Cleveland, E. J., and Longaker, W. D. Neurotic patterns in the family. In A. Leighton, J. A. Clausen and R. N. Wilson (Eds.), *Explorations in social psychiatry.* New York: Basic Books, 1957. Pp. 167–200.

Cousins, A. N. The failure of solidarity. In N. W. Bell & E. F. Vogel (Eds.), *A modern introduction to the family.* Glencoe, Ill.: Free Press, 1960. Pp. 403–416.

Eisenstein, V. W. (Ed.) *Neurotic interaction in marriage.* New York: Basic Books, 1956.

Elles, G. W. The closed circuit: The study of a delinquent family. *British Journal of Criminology,* 1961, 2, 23–39.

Escalona, Sibylle, and Heider, Grace. *Prediction and outcome: A study in child development.* New York: Basic Books, 1959.

Escalona, Sibylle, and Leitch, Mary. Early phases of personality development. *Monographs of the Society for Research in Child Development,* 1952, *17,* (1, Whole No. 54).

Fisher, S., and Mendell, D. The communication of neurotic patterns over two and three generations. *Psychiatry,* 1956, *10,* 41–46.

Fisher, S., and Mendell, D. The spread of psychotherapeutic effects from the patient to his family group. *Psychiatry,* 1958, *21,* 133–140.

Flavell, J. H. Some observations on schizophrenic thinking: Observation and onset. *Canadian Journal of Psychology,* 1957, *11,* 128–132.

Fleck, S. Family dynamics and origin of schizophrenia. *Psychosomatic Medicine,* 1960, 22, 333–344.

Fleck, S., Lidz, T., Cornelison, Alice, Schafer, Sarah, and Terry, Dorothy. The intrafamilial environment of the schizophrenic patient: Incestuous and homosexual dynamics. In J. H. Masserman (Ed.), *Individual and familial dynamics.* New York: Grune and Stratton, 1959. Pp. 142–159.

Freeman, V. J., Klein, A. F., Riehman, Lynne, Lukoff, I. F., and Heisey, Virginia. "Family group counseling" as differentiated from other family therapies. *International Journal of Group Psychotherapy,* 1963, *13,* 167–175.

Frenkel-Brunswik, Else. Differential patterns of social outlook and personality in family and children. In Margaret Mead and Martha Wolfenstein (Eds.), *Childhood in contemporary cultures.* Chicago: University of Chicago Press, 1955. Pp. 369–402.

Fries, Margaret, and Woolf, P. J. Some hypotheses on the role of the congenital activity type in personality development. *Psychoanalytic Study of the Child,* 1954, *8,* 48–62.

Getzels, J. W., and Jackson, P. *Creativity and intelligence.* New York: Wiley, 1962.

Goffman, E. *Encounters: Two studies in the sociology of interaction.* Indianapolis, Ind.: Bobbs-Merrill, 1961.

Grotjahn, M. Analytic family therapy: A survey of trends in research and practice. In J. Masserman (Ed.), *Individual and familial dynamics.* New York: Grune and Stratton, 1959. Pp. 90–104.

Grotjahn, M. *Psychoanalysis and the family neurosis.* New York: Norton, 1960.

Group for the Advancement of Psychiatry. *Integration and conflict in family relations.* (Report No. 27) Topeka, Kans.: GAP, 1954.

Haley, J. The family of the schizophrenic: A model system. *Journal of Nervous and Mental Disease,* 1959, *129,* 357–374. (a)

Haley, J. An interactional description of schizophrenia. *Psychiatry,* 1959, *22,* 321–332. (b)

Haley, J. Family experiments: A new type of experimentation. *Family Process,* 1962, 1, 265–293.

Handel, G. A study of family and personality. Unpublished doctoral dissertation, University of Chicago, 1962.

Handel, G., and Hess, R. D. The family as an emotional organization. *Marriage and Family Living,* 1956, *18,* 99–101.

Harris, I. *Normal children and mothers.* Glencoe, Ill.: Free Press, 1959.

Henry, J. Family structure and the transmission of neurotic behavior. *American Journal of Orthopsychiatry,* 1951, *21,* 800–818.

Henry, J., and Warson, S. Family structure and psychic development. *American Journal of Orthopsychiatry,* 1951, *21,* 59–73.

Henry, W. E. The thematic apperception technique in the study of group and cultural problems. In H. H. Anderson and G. L. Anderson (Eds.), *An introduction to projective techniques.* New York: Prentice-Hall, 1951. Pp. 230–278.

Henry, W. E. *The analysis of fantasy.* New York: Wiley, 1956.

Henry, W. E., and Guetzkow, H. Group projection sketches for the study of small groups. *Journal of Social Psychology,* 1951, *33,* 77–102.

Hess, R. D., and Handel, G. *Family worlds. A psychosocial approach to family life.* Chicago: University of Chicago Press, 1959.

Hill, R. *Families under stress: Adjustment to the crises of war separation and reunion.* New York: Harper, 1949.

Hoffman, Lois, and Lippitt, R. The measurement of family life variables. In P. H. Mussen (Ed.), *Handbook of research methods in child development.* New York: Wiley, 1960. Pp. 945–1013.

Jackson, D. D. The question of family homeostasis. Part 1. *Psychiatric Quarterly Supplement,* 1957, *31,* 79–90.

Jackson, D. D. Family interaction, family homeostasis and some implications for conjoint family therapy. In J. H. Masserman (Ed.), *Individual and familial dynamics.* New York: Grune and Stratton, 1959. Pp. 122–141.

Jackson, D. D. Family therapy in the family of the schizophrenic. In M. I. Stein (Ed.), *Contemporary psychotherapies.* New York: Free Press of Glencoe, 1961. Pp. 272–287.

Jackson, D. D., Riskin, J., and Satir, Virginia. A method of analysis of a family interview. *Archives of General Psychiatry,* 1961, *5,* 321–339.

Jackson, D. D., and Weakland, J. Schizophrenic symptoms and family interaction. *Archives of General Psychiatry,* 1959, *1,* 618–621.

Jackson, D. D., and Weakland, J. Conjoint family therapy: Some considerations on theory, technique and results. *Psychiatry,* 1961, *24* (2, Suppl.), 30–45.

Josslyn, Irene. The family as a psychological unit. *Social Casework,* 1953, *34,* 336–343.

Kaplan, B. *Studying personality cross-culturally.* Evanston, Ill.: Row, Peterson, 1961.

Kluckhohn, C., and Murray, H. A. *Personality in nature, society and culture.* New York: Knopf, 1948.

Kluckhohn, Florence. Dominant substitute profiles of cultural orientations: Their significance for the analysis of social stratification. *Social Forces,* 1950, *28,* 276–293.

Leichter, Hope J. Boundaries of the family as an empirical and theoretical unit. In N. W. Ackerman, Frances L. Beatman, and S. N. Sherman (Eds.), *Exploring the base for family therapy.* New York: Family Service Association, 1961. Pp. 140–144.

Lewin, K., Lippitt, R., and White, R. K. Patterns of aggressive behavior in experimentally created "social climates." *Journal of Social Psychology,* 1939, *10,* 271–299.

Lewis, O. An anthropological approach to family studies. *American Journal of Sociology,* 1950, *55,* 468–475.

Lewis, O. *Five families: Mexican case studies in the culture of poverty.* New York: Basic Books, 1959.

Lewis, O. *The children of Sanchez.* New York: Random House, 1961.

Lidz, T., Cornelison, Alice, Fleck, S., and Terry, Dorothy. The intrafamilial environment of the schizophrenic patient: II. Marital schism and marital skew. *American Journal of Psychiatry,* 1957, *114,* 241–248.

Lidz, T., Cornelison, Alice, Terry, Dorothy, and Fleck, S. Intrafamilial environment of the schizophrenic patient: VI. The transmission of irrationality. *Archives of Neurology and Psychiatry,* 1958, *79,* 305–316.

Lidz, T., Fleck, S., Cornelison, Alice, and Terry, Dorothy. Intrafamilial environment of the schizophrenic patient: IV. Parental personalities and family interaction. *American Journal of Orthopsychiatry,* 1958, *28,* 764–776.

Lu, Yi-chuang. Mother-child role ralationships in schizophrenia: A comparison of schizophrenic patients with non-schizophrenic siblings. *Psychiatry,* 1961, *24,* 133–142.

Mead, Margaret. *Coming of age in Samoa.* New York: Morrow, 1928.

Mendell, D., and Fisher, S. An approach to neurotic behavior in terms of a three-generation family model. *Journal of Nervous and Mental Disease,* 1956, *123,* 171–180.

Mendell, D., and Fisher, S. A multi-generation approach to treatment of psychopathology. *Journal of Nervous and Mental Disease,* 1958, *126,* 523–529.

Miller, D. Personality and social interaction. In B. Kaplan (Ed.), *Studying personality cross-culturally.* Evanston, Ill.: Row, Peterson, 1961. Pp. 271–298.

Mittelman, B. Complementary neurotic reactions in intimate relationships. *Psychoanalytic Quarterly,* 1944, *13,* 479–491.

Mittelman, B. The concurrent analysis of married couples. *Psychoanalytic Quarterly,* 1948, *17,* 182–197.

Murphy, Lois. *The widening world of childhood.* New York: Basic Books, 1962.

Neiman, L. J., and Hughes, J. W. The problem of the concept of role: A re-survey of the literature. *Social Forces,* 1951, *30,* 141–149.

Oberndorf, C. P. Psychoanalysis of married couples. *Psychoanalytic Review,* 1938, *25,* 453–465.

Parsons, T., and Bales, R. F. *Family, socialization and interaction process.* Glencoe, Ill.: Free Press, 1955.

Powdermaker, Florence. Concepts found useful in the treatment of schizoid and ambulatory schizophrenic patients. *Psychiatry,* 1952, *15,* 61–71.

Redl, F. Group emotion and leadership. *Psychiatry,* 1942, *5,* 573–596.

Robb, L. H. Experiences with ordinary families. *British Journal of Medical Psychology,* 1953, *26,* 215–221.

Roberts, J. M. Three Navaho households: A comparative study in small group culture. *Papers of the Peabody Museum of American Archaeology and Ethnology, Harvard University,* 1951, *40,* (3).

Rose, A. A systematic summary of symbolic interaction theory. In A. Rose (Ed.), *Human behavior and social processes.* Boston, Mass.: Houghton Mifflin, 1962. Pp. 3–19.

Rosenzweig, S., and Cass, L. K. The extension of psychodiagnosis to parents in the child guidance setting. *American Journal of Orthopsychiatry,* 1954, *24,* 715–722.

Rosenzweig, S., and Isham, A. C. Complementary Thematic Apperception Test patterns in close kin. *American Journal of Orthopsychiatry,* 1947, *17,* 129–142.

Ryckoff, I., Day, J., and Wynne, L. C. Maintenance of stereotyped roles in the families of schizophrenics. *Archives of General Psychiatry,* 1959, *1,* 109–114.

Sarbin, T. R. Role theory. In G. Lindzey (Ed.), *Handbook of social psychology.* Vol. 1. Cambridge, Mass.: Addison-Wesley, 1954. Pp. 223–258.

Sargent, S. S. Conceptions of role and ego in contemporary psychology. In J. H. Rohrer and M. Sherif (Eds.), *Social psychology at the crossroads.* New York: Harper, 1951.

Sherif, M. *The psychology of social norms.* New York: Harper, 1936.

Sohler, Dorothy Terry, Holzberg, J. D., Fleck, S., Cornelison, Alice, Kay, Eleanor, and Lidz, T. The prediction of family interaction from a battery of projective tests. *Journal of Projective Techniques,* 1957, *21,* 199–208.

Spiegel, J., and Bell, N. W. The family of the psychiatric patient. In S. Arieti (Ed.), *American handbook of psychiatry.* New York: Basic Books, 1959. Pp. 114–149.

Strodtbeck, F. L. The family as a three-person group. *American Sociological Review,* 1954, *19,* 23–29.

Strodtbeck, F. L. Family interaction, values and achievement. In D. McClelland, A. Baldwin, U. Bronfenbrenner, and F. L. Strodtbeck, *Talent and society.* Princeton, N. J.: Van Nostrand, 1958. Pp. 135–194.

Tharp, R. Psychological patterning in marriage. *Psychological Bulletin,* 1963, *60,* 97–117.

Titchener, J., Riskin, J., and Emerson, R. The family in psychosomatic process: A case report illustrating a method of psychosomatic research. *Psychosomatic Medicine,* 1960, *22,* 127–142.

Vogel, E. F., and Bell, N. W. The emotionally disturbed child as the family scapegoat. In N. W. Bell and E. F. Vogel (Eds.), *A modern introduction to the family.* Glencoe, Ill.: Free Press, 1960.

Voiland, A. L. *Family casework diagnosis.* New York: Columbia University Press, 1962.

Weakland, J. H. The "double-bind" hypothesis of schizophrenia and three-party interaction. In D. D. Jackson (Ed.), *The etiology of schizophrenia.* New York: Basic Books, 1960. Pp. 373–388.

White, R. Abnormalities of behavior. *Annual Review of Psychology*, 1959, *10,* 265–286.

Wynne, L. C. The study of intrafamilial alignments and splits in exploratory family therapy. In N. W. Ackerman, Frances L. Beatman, and S. N. Sherman (Eds.), *Exploring the base for family therapy.* New York: Family Service Association, 1961. Pp. 95–115.

Wynne, L. C., Ryckoff, I. M., Day, Juliana, and Hirsch, S. I. Pseudo-mutuality in the family relations of schizophrenics. *Psychiatry,* 1958, *21,* 205–220.

7

The Individual and
the Larger Contexts

DON D. JACKSON

We are on the edge of a new era in psychiatry and the related disciplines of psychology, social work, anthropology and sociology. In this new era we will come to look at human nature in a much more complex way than ever before. From this threshold the view is not of the individual *in vitro* but of the small or larger group within which any particular individual's behavior is adaptive. We will move from individual assessment to analysis of the contexts, or more precisely, the *system* from which individual conduct is inseparable.

Now this is obviously a very recondite area, one in which a beginning is just being made in family research, utilizing a patchwork of systems theory, cybernetics and information theory, but I think there is a great promise that this group-oriented approach will tremendously enhance our knowledge of human behavior. Further, the conceptual problems we face in family

From *Family Process*, Vol. 6, No. 2, September 1967, pp. 139–154.

study are shared by students of political, biological, and even artificial or inorganic systems, so there is a situation, rare and exciting in science, in which we can seek broad theoretical solutions of vital interest to incredibly diverse fields of study. At the moment, however, let us examine a few of the issues which arise when the family system of an individual is studied.

For over ten years I have been studying family interaction to see whether and how such interaction relates to psychopathology or deviant behavior in one or more family members. For the past five years a group at the Mental Research Institute in Palo Alto has been studying the "normal" as well as the "disturbed" family in order to have some base line for the pathological. Our approach has been interaction-oriented because we believe that individual personality, character and deviance are shaped by the individual's relations with his fellows. As Shibutani has stated:

> many of the things men do take a certain form not so much from instincts as from the necessity of adjusting to their fellows. What characterizes the interactionist approach is the contention that human nature and the social order are products of communication . . . the direction taken by a person's conduct is seen as something that is constructed in the reciprocal give and take of interdependent men who are adjusting to one another. Furthermore, a man's personality—those distinctive behavior patterns that characterize a given individual—is regarded as developing and being reaffirmed from day to day in his interaction with his associates (italics omitted).[1]

We view symptoms, defenses, character structure, and personality as terms describing the individual's typical interactions which occur in response to a particular interpersonal context, rather than as intrapsychic entities. Since the family is the most influential learning context, surely a more detailed study of family process will yield valuable clues to the etiology of such typical modes of interaction. Whether one thinks in terms of "role," "tactics," or "behavior repertoire," it is obvious that the individual is shaped by, and in turn helps to shape, his family. This may not at first appear to be such a startlingly new approach but rather the most commonplace social psychology or, at best merely a shift of emphasis, an accentuation of ideas which are implicit in many of the great theories of contemporary behavioral science which refer to "interaction," "relationships," etc. But it has been our experience, which I want to share with you, that when one begins to approach or even gather the data, it makes all the difference in the world exactly where the primary emphasis lies. One finds oneself almost immediately faced with certain conceptual watersheds, certain discontinuities between interactional data and individual theories. I would like to discuss two of these critical problems.

The first is the question of the basic unit of study: is it the "individual" or the system as what L. K. Frank called an *"organized complexity"?* Operating from the interactionist view, our original approach to the family was, and somewhat unavoidably has continued to be, the search for common processes in families with a schizophrenic, a delinquent, an asthmatic, or other "abnormal" *individual* member. My dissatisfaction comes from the fact that, although this investigation of the influences of the family on the individual patient has yielded many new and useful concepts, hunches and observations, it also contains inherent difficulties and potential fallacies. We must remain constantly alert to the dangers inherent in using an individual as a starting point from which to investigate family interaction data.

Especially if we use the symptom as our starting point, our problem is immediately that the psychiatric nosology or system for labeling deviance is almost totally individual-oriented, not at all well suited to considering the *interpersonal context* in which the patient's behavior takes place. The absence of psychiatric labeling, which is our only referent for normality, only seemingly avoids this inadequacy, for on consideration it is the same problem in converse. Further, the inadequacies of individual classification schemes can only lead to compounded confusion in family classification.

These pitfalls have led us to a few ground rules about interactional research, especially in regard to the concept of the individual. First, though our practical and clinical interests may be served by classifying families according to the presence or absence of individual pathology, we must avoid imposing the elements of individual theory onto the family model. That is, there is no evidence for the isomorphy of the two theoretical models. The shift from individual to interactional thinking may be a discontinuous one in psychiatry, and we must scrupulously examine the basic premises and methods of the former model before applying it to the latter. *It is likely that what we mean by the term "individual" when we take the family system into account may be quite different from what this term presently describes.* It is unlikely that a typology of families as systems will simply be able to use individual nosology. Specifically, we must not let our desire to understand and to ameliorate individual pathology carry us into family process with individual-oriented theories, lest we do disservice to both theory and therapy. This error has two forms: we might treat the family as only an additive compound of its individual members and neglect the transactions and the whole; or, out of habit, we might encase these members in hypothetical skin and apply to this unit the theoretical models of the individual.

In the second place, the tendency to these kinds of errors leads us to examine not only our theories of family structure, but more basically, our philosophy of causality. The behavioral sciences are only now coming to the transition made by many of the natural sciences in this century, i.e., from a mechanical to a systems theory. Specifically, our traditional model of causality does not encompass those feedback processes of a system which *achieve outcomes.* The problem of like causes which do not produce like results (or, conversely, identical results from unlike antecedents) has been analyzed in cybernetics in terms of positive and negative feedback mechanisms. A random event introduced into a system with deviation-amplifying tendencies, for instance, will produce a final result quite different from the same event in a system with deviation-counteracting processes. Thus the study of single elements or static "before and after" situations will not be too enlightening.

Neither, then, is the study of essentially accidental historical events feasible. Adopting the premise of the family as a system requires us to *attend only to present(observable) process*, that is, to ecology rather than genesis.

The circular, or feedback, model of causality is a necessary corollary to our basic axioms of communication. It is impossible to think in terms of interpersonal systems with the ordinary cause-and-effect notions. The strictly individual point of view tends to minimize the two-way effect of persons on each other.

These assumptions have enormous influence on the daily practice of psychiatry, on parents' attitudes toward various child-rearing practices, and on those most important of citizens, our educators. It is not uncommon to encounter a schizophrenic who has been denied a possible chance of recovery by the psychiatrist's attitude toward the label "schizophrenia" as a heredito-constitutional thought disorder. The label is framed by the parents' earnest willingness to supply various details that demonstrate that the disorder was present from birth. Our research group noted that in twenty-one of twenty-two first interviews with the parents of a group of young schizophrenics, head injury and the school systems were uniformly mentioned by the parents as important causative factors.

What seems like ordinary common sense can also lead us astray. If we remember John as a little boy, especially if he used to be a trouble-making little stinker, and we see John twenty years later in the clutches of the law, we are apt to be impressed with the fixity of the human character and the infant molding which has occurred. We may forget to be impressed with the fixity of the system within which John lived. The variation of responses permissible within this system may be small and those responses which the social sieve quickly filters out might bring John to the attention of its agencies. Or we may forget that certain other kids were also stinkers at John's age but turned out to be decent God-fearing adults. In fact, there have been a few studies of normal subjects who reported traumatic backgrounds essentially similar to those of the general run of analytic patients with neurotic disorders. If we exclude the *clichés* of genetic predisposition, the only explanation for such differences lies in family and social processes, in those vital relationships where the trauma is amplified or counteracted.

Maruyama, in a personal communication, points out that by a "deviation-amplifying mutual causal process" a relatively small kick can be enlarged by the system over time to sizable deviations. In this light, the difference between the environment of identical twins does not have to be large in order finally to produce sizeable differences between them. He also points out that a small set of rules can generate a very complex pattern. This might be important to the family rules, because some will be more vulnerable to mutual deviation-amplifying effects than others. He states further that it requires much *more* information to go from the adult pattern back to the embryo than to study the rules of the embryo and understand how it becomes adult. This has relevance to the historical method in psychiatry, where inferences and implications are made about the adult state based on assumptions about what the early state must have been.

Finally, in this question of the appropriate model of causality, it must be emphasized that the linear, cause-and-effect train goes by only once, and once past, is incapable of being retrieved. The accumulation of evidence is that self-or-parent-reported histories are notoriously unreliable, filtering the past through the present as well as through the selective vagaries of human memory. Whatever an individual says about his past is also a comment on, or way of handling, the interviewer; that is, the "history" is a metaphor about the present relationship. Such methods, therefore, make impossible the distinction between cause and effect which they seek to clarify. The same charge, incidentally, must be leveled at an unfortunately large amount of present family research which, though purporting to study interaction, actually applies standard individual testing methods to individuals who happen to be related. The impossible question must logically be asked of such research: are the family members such and such a way because one member is ill or is that member ill because the other family members are the way they are and, presumably, were when the patient was born? Only the study of the family as a contemporary, ongoing system with circular networks of interaction can avoid this pointless and irresolvable debate.

All this is not merely armchair philosophy. It is my contention that psychiatry must consider such systems analysis if it is going to fulfill its present obligations and open up new possibilities in the improvement of psychotherapeutic intervention. If, for example, a psychiatrist interviews a couple who complain of marital difficulty, he might describe the wife as hypochondriacal, ineffectual, dependent, with hysterical tendencies, and the husband as cold, efficient, passive-aggressive, etc. Short of sending them immediately to an attorney, his recommendation is apt to be based on the notion that "each" of these individuals is disturbed and will require a good deal of therapy if he is to live with the other. However, there is another way of looking at this particular couple. They can be viewed as a mutual causative system, whose complementary communication reinforces the nature of their interaction. The therapist can look for rules that govern this system; therapy then consists of the therapist behaving in such a way that the rules must change. Rather than focusing on individual pathology, he might notice that this couple behaves in a remarkably consistent manner, the paradigm of which might be:

The wife demands, in any one of dozens of possible ways, that the husband love her. (Paradoxical, since "love" has to be spontaneous.)

The husband replies tangentially, or perfunctorily, that he does.

Wife is enraged and refuses his message, saying she doesn't need it anyway.

Husband is hurt and withdraws. (Paradoxical in the framework of marriage.)

Wife responds by demanding he love her, and the game begins again.

If you will accept my description of this couple's interaction as no less accurate or more inferential than the usual psychiatric formulation, then let us consider some of the differences in emphasis from a more traditional view.

(*a*) Neither is more wrong, or sick, than the other, and thus could be said to "start things." The wife's paradoxical command, "Love me," is of course impossible to respond to appropriately; but the husband's withdrawal within the context of marriage, which therefore amounts to a denial that he is *really* withdrawing, is equally impossible to decipher and deal with.

(*b*) It matters little how this got started, since once under way it tends to be self-perpetuating and mutually causative. The responses each makes are about the only ones available to them, and the longer the process continues, the more rigidly such responses will be made, thus inevitably triggering the sequence.

(*c*) Individual psychiatric symptoms can be seen as functional, even necessary, in such a system. Psychosomatic symptoms on the part of the wife would engender the husband's solicitude and involvement; or a third party, one of the children, might become such a problem that the parents are brought into a coalition in order to deal with him and are able to focus all their difficulties on him. The important point here is that the behavior which is usually seen as symptomatic in terms of the individual can be seen as adaptive, even appropriate, in terms of the vital system within which the individual operates.

It may be protested at this point that our present theories supply us with terms such as "sado-masochistic symbiosis" to describe the above, and perhaps any other, two-party relationship. However, I feel such a term is not useful because it reductionistically obscures the important elements of causality. Such a formulation implies that a sadist met a masochist and they lived happily ever after because they were "made for each other." On the contrary, we are constantly defining and *being defined by* the nature of our relationships. (Another objection to this particular description of a relationship is the connotation of force and morality attached to any of the "domination" words. The power of passivity has been demonstrated to us from Christ to Gandhi and the present success of "sit-ins," and we must begin to consider the many levels of communication other than overt individual power seeking which control the nature of relationships.)

In examining the role of the individual within a system, I have relied thus far on examples from the family, surely a vital, virtually universal, yet readily investigable interpersonal unit. Let us expand this kind of analysis to international systems with an example from the philosopher, C. E. M. Joad:

> if, as they maintain, the best way to preserve peace is to prepare war, it is not altogether clear why all nations should regard the armaments of other nations as a menace to peace. However, they do so regard them, and are accordingly stimulated to increase their armaments to overtop the armaments by which they cenceive themselves to be threatened . . . These increased arms being in their turn regarded as a menace by nation A whose allegedly defensive armaments have provoked them, are used by nation A as a pretext for accumulating yet greater armaments wherewith to defend itself against the menace. These yet greater armaments are in turn interpreted by neighboring nations as constituting a menace to themselves and so on. . . .[2]

This form of analysis makes it clear that the behavior of nation A stimulates the behavior of nation B, which in turn spurs on nation A, such escalation being abetted by one-sightedness on the parts of both nations who see only their individual *reactions* and not their mutual roles in an extremely dangerous system.

We know that the Wright brothers flew roughly 100 yards at Kittyhawk in 1908, and today men travel in 1700-mile-per-hour jets. This is progress; it is sure and almost dull and commonplace. However, progress in psychiatry is never thought of in such terms, because we don't know in what direction to head or how to get there. That is, we cannot expand what we now have and consider it progress. Ten thousand psychiatrists doing what a thousand are now doing will result in increased coverage but little progress. To fulfill its promise, psychiatry must develop a frame of reference that is supraindividual while retaining its traditional model as well. Einstein did not nullify the work of Clerk-Maxwell, but his frame of reference represented a spectacular departure from his predecessors. We can keep our traditional ideas about individual motivation and personality and learn also to examine contexts. This sort of tolerance has been necessary in other, more "scientific" fields. Several years ago the Quaker mathematician, Lewis Fry Richardson, had this to say when he noticed that the outbreaks of wars throughout history follow simply and precisely a well know statistical formula, the Poisson distribution:

> This explanation of the occurrence of wars is certainly far removed from such explanations as ordinarily appear in newspapers, including the protracted and critical negotiations, the inordinate ambition and the hideous perfidy of the opposing statesmen, and the suspect movements of their armed personnel. The two types of explanations are, however, not necessarily contradictory; they can be reconciled by saying that each can separately be true as far as it goes, but cannot be the whole truth. A similar diversity of explanation occurs in regard to marriage: on the one hand we have the impersonal and moderately constant marriage rate; on the other hand we have the intense and fluctuating personal emotions of a love-story; yet both types of description can be true.[3]

As psychiatrists, we cannot view diverse theories in an "either-or" fashion but must live with the idea that many discontinuous approaches should be investigated and given credence.

Thus, all this is not to deny individuality as a value nor to belittle the importance of the subjective experience of ourselves as individuals. I mean rather to emphasize a new dimension in the study of human behavior, an interactional perspective which all who would involve themselves in the affairs of mankind have a responsibility to recognize. Attention to the individual in the extreme is artificial and cannot be the basis for realistic actions. Recently, the Nobel Prize-winning geneticist,

H. J. Muller, proposed a eugenic program which would "aim at the ideals of *intelligence, creativity, cooperative temperament, joy of life, vigor* and *perceptivity* that have allowed men to reach their present high position" (italics mine).[4] I feel all the qualities which Dr. Muller cites as individual properties take form and meaning only in interaction and are in fact inseparable from the persons with whom the individual is involved. One who is joyful in isolation is very likely to find himself taken to a mental hospital. We have the enormous job of translating such intuitively obvious notions into precise scientific language.

REFERENCES

1. Shibutani, T. *Society and personality.* Englewood Cliffs, N.J.: Prentice-Hall, 1961, p. 20.
2. Joad, C. E. M. *Why war?* Penguin Special, 1939, p. 69.
3. Richardson, L. F. Statistics of deadly quarrels, in J. R. Newman (Ed.), *The world of mathematics*, Vol. 2. New York: Simon and Schuster, 1956. p. 1258.
4. Muller, H. J., Perspectives for the life sciences. *Bull. Atomic Scientists,* January 3–7, 1964.

DISCUSSION

GEORGE VASSILIOU

I will gladly comment on Dr. Jackson's paper since at the Athenian Institute of Anthropos we are operating on the ideas expressed in his opening statement. Currently[1] we are presenting data concerning transaction within the Greek family, which illustrate exactly the point that the individual should not be examined *in vitro* but within the context of the group in which he lives and within his total sociocultural milieu. The subject under discussion there is the significance of the dependence that the Greek family fosters. Our research data concerning variables related to family transaction such as husband-wife relations, parent–child relations, family roles, attitudes, stereotypes, child–rearing practices, maternal intervention in peer group formation, patterns of diciplining children, investigated on the basis of samples representative of the general urban population, indicate that the Greek family indeed does *foster dependence*. This is supported by motivational patterns of 12-year-old and 18-year-old normal achieving adolescents as detected by Story Sequence Analysis which show them as being definitely on the dependence pole of the dependence–independence dimension. Reviewers of these findings tend to conclude that this kind of family is a "sick family," that we deal with a "sick culture." These reviewers, as we have repeated in a formal occasion recently,[2] examine things *in vitro*. They do not take under consideration at all the sociocultural matricies within which these family patterns have been developed for centuries exactly because they have a high adaptational value. As further research, supported significantly from cross-cultural studies,[3] has shown, in the Greek milieu the In-Group (defined as family, friends and friends of friends) is perceived as a "mothering" entity with a highly nurturant and supportive role comparable only to mother-child role. Progress in life, from sheer biological survival onwards, depends on the skill of the individual in securing and actualizing interdependencies in his life. Conclusion: we deal with patterns which cannot be qualified as adaptive or maladaptive but which can be evaluated only in the context of the group and the milieu in which the individual lives. Such conclusions should have been obvious if psychiatry in the late sixties were not still permeated by the most progressive thinking of the past century. The discussant can only agree with melancholy with the conclusion of the writer that behavioral sciences are following the natural sciences with a lag of fifty years. It seems though that we are finally overcoming our intellectual inertia. We are entering a stage in which mental reactions are viewed as multifactorial. Biological, intrapsychic, interpersonal, intergroup and sociocultural variables are perceived not as mutually exclusive causative factors but as processes developing in a multilateral transaction. Nevertheless, in trying to overcome reductionism we should keep in mind that one of the reinforcements of reductionism is the inevitable need for the clinician to focus on something circumscribed in order to function diagnostically and therapeutically. Clinicians using general systems theory will inevitably feel the same need and they will "focus." We agree with the writer that it makes a tremendous difference on what one *focuses* in clinical practice. We want only to stress something which we hope that he shares: that the clinician will always keep in mind that he is "focusing" and that by doing so he leaves at the moment much out of his scope and his therapeutic maneuvers.

If we let systems theory be perceived as a polar opposite of psychodynamic theories which are trying to explain the individual and the interpersonal phenomena as *nothing but* an affirmative multiplication of the individual processes, we run the risk of developing not a new approach to the study of psychiatric phenomena, but an equally dangerous one-sidedness which this time might be called abstractionism, in contradistinction to reductionism.

To be more specific, symptoms, defenses, etc., should not be viewed as terms of interpersonal transaction *or* intrapsychic entities. These two views of one and the same phenomenon should not be understood and described as mutually exclusive, but as complementary. We agree with the writer that as clinicians we have to focus on some part of the continuum each time, and our emphasis on which part of the continuum we focus influences heavily (and so often untherapeutically) our practice. It is not despite, but because of this that we do not want to perpetuate dichotomies. We feel that Dr. Jackson agrees with us, but we feel obliged to make certain points more explicit because we have already started experiencing the danger of seeing the whole effort to which he has contributed so much going astray.

Ecology is as important as genesis. If two different processes *A* and *B*, examined ecologically, are found to produce the same result *X*, biogenetics and psychogenetics are important in contributing to our understanding of the intrinsic differences between them. In turn, the understanding of their exact differences will eventually contribute to the understanding of possible intervening processes, amplifying or counteracting.

Given that in each interpersonal encounter two *different* personalities transact, we feel that autobiographic "material" is as valuable, as the observable "here and now" transaction. Not because we find it "objective" but exactly because its alterations, being related to the other each time, illuminate aspects of the transaction. Focusing on the present or the past exclusively will eventually introduce limitations.

Personally, we accept, on the basis of overall logistics related to the available time of the therapist, that it is more economical to focus and deal with observable patterns of transaction developing "here and now." But we do this really to integrate the historical dimension as well. Genetics become of course a largely meaningless museum document, if examined independently of the dynamics of the given interpersonal field. But on the other hand, dynamics lose much of their significant, *personal* meaning if examined independently of genetics. After all the constant re-writing of the past by the individual, the sequence of its variations, are "genetics" revealing much about dynamics.

It is undeniable that reductionism in the behavioral sciences has led to dehumanization. General systems theory can be easily misunderstood, misapplied and made to lead to a polar opposite of reductionism, an abstractionism, with equally dehumanizing effects.

It is not advisable at all to reverse the pendulum if we are going to take it to the other end. We have to keep it in balance, otherwise we are going to develop a "Psychiatry of the Absurd," a psychiatry based on reductionistic or abstractionistic approaches. And this will inevitably happen if we forget the very essence of systems theory, which is complementarity and synthesis, and if we attempt instead to counteract reductionism by adopting its polar opposites, by perpetuating artificial dichotomies and by insisting on mutually exclusive concepts.

To the above comments Don D. Jackson answered as follows:

"Dr. Vassiliou's remarks are penetrating and his admonitions are well taken. In fact, I can find nothing to disagree with in his comments and am glad, for this reason, that I hope to study at his institute next year."

Alas! this hope was never fulfilled. Don D. Jackson left us all, prematurely and suddenly. A verse of one of the greatest modern Greek poets, Costis Palamas, speaks succinctly for Don and his life's work:
    . . . and the reflection's depths like the action's breadths."
Given that, he could have repeated with St. Exupéry's Little Prince:
    "I shall look as if I were dead; and that will not be true. . . ."

NATHAN B. EPSTEIN

Those of us who know Don Jackson through personal contact and/or his writings are aware that he is a brilliant, erudite, articulate man who writes clearly and lucidly. In his research work he demonstrates an unusual sensitivity to the nuances of communication in human interaction and knowledge of a number of conceptual systems applicable to behaviour. The conceptual systems to which he refers most frequently in his work are general systems theory, cybernetics, communication theory, interactional theory and psychodynamic theory. All of these qualities are demonstrated quite clearly in this paper on which I have been asked to comment.

There is yet another quality manifested in the paper, a quality frequently associated with the role of pioneer, and a pioneer in the field of family psychiatry Don Jackson certainly is. This quality is that of advocate or "pitchman" (in this instance an extremely eloquent one). It appears in the first of the two distinct parts of which this paper is composed and leads the author to disregard his own advice given in the second portion of the paper (the last eighth) where he states: "As psychiatrists, we cannot view diverse theories in an 'either-or' fashion, but must live with the idea that many discontinuous approaches should be investigated and given credence."

In the paper Jackson makes the "big pitch" for the study of the individual within the context of the groups in which he operates. This is a laudable directive. The only quarrel I have with it is the manner in which it is made—in the first seventh-eighths of the paper. In this portion he presents the various theoretic approaches in dichotomous either-or terms, with one side being "good" and the other "bad," and only fit for the ash can.

The dichotomies as presented in categorical and dogmatic terms include:

1. The social sciences of psychology, social work, anthropology and sociology vs. (by implication) the "harder" natural and physical sciences as genetics, neurophysiology, neuropharmacology, neurochemistry, psychoendocrinology, etc.

2. The study of the system vs. study of the individual, or only a portion of him.

3. The systems approach to causality vs. the mechanical.

4. The study of present process vs. past genesis.

The positions acceptable to the author are presented first in my above list.

Such dogmatic advocacy has the useful function of alerting students and workers to approaches hitherto ignored or unknown. There are several inherent dangers, including: throwing the baby out with the wash; encouraging polemical debate rather than scientific discussion based upon presentation of *facts* gathered by well designed and conceived studies based upon well defined hypotheses arising out of various conceptual systems or theoretical models.

Those of us involved in the study of human behaviour are not in a position to disregard any approach that might prove useful for purposes of investigation. Our colleagues and students should be encouraged to become conversive with all available approaches, and to learn how to apply them in an objective, scientific manner. The primary problem facing us is the development of satisfactory techniques of scientific investigation. Unnecessary polemics merely serve as time-wasting, energy-draining diversions.

Jackson obviously recognizes this in the final segment of this paper when he returns to the scientific position. He is too fine a behavioural scientist to stray too far too long. There are many roads to the "Promised Land."

LYMAN C. WYNNE

I am sorry that Dr. Jackson did not reread and edit this paper more carefully. At the beginning, he roars down what appears to be a one-way street, with sirens blaring, as if he had the one worthwhile objective in mind (the study of family systems) and the one reliable means of getting there (observation of ongoing family process).

The first question he raises is in either-or terms: whether "*the* basic unit of study" is "the 'individual' *or* the system" (italics mine). Up to the concluding paragraphs, he gives no hint that in his view "individuals" can *also* be regarded as systems in their own right. At most, he concedes that his attention to individual family members has continued "somewhat unavoidably" to serve "practical and clinical interests"— certainly not as a legitimate conceptual and methodologic alternative.

Knowing Don Jackson personally, I did not believe he believed what he appeared to be saying. This supposition turned out to be right. At the end, he graciously suggests that psychiatry may retain "its traditional model *as well as* developing a supra-individual one, and that "as psychiatrists, we cannot view diverse theories in an 'either-or' fashion"—a rather startling reversal of the earlier pages.

Without lauching into a lengthy paper of my own, I suggest that a more comprehensive and thoroughgoing systems theory is in order, based upon the principle of *open linked* systems, in which two (but not the only two) systems which can be linked are individual personality systems and family systems. Using this formulation, the family as a system may be a distinctive starting point, but so is individual personality. (In the last few years, as the result of cross-cultural observations, I am more impressed than I once was with the many circumstances and contexts in which families do *not* behave as systems. But more of that on another occasion.)

Obviously, no open system can be adequately described—or hardly described at all!—without detailed attention to its transactions with other systems, for examples, personalities with other personalities, personalities with families, families with families. The *"typical"* transactions of an individual or a family are then used, always merely as a convenient abstraction or generalization, to characterize that individual or that family. To be sure, some clinicians and researchers do get caught up with a concretized, reified belief in some kind of ultimate "reality" which they see in their own abstractions. This has happened with distinguished writers in many fields. Many a Freudian analyst has implicitly come to believe in the little men of ego, id, and superego, warring, wooing, and compromising in their intrapsychic domain. However, I hope that we do not think we are improving our theories if we turn the rascals out only to replace them in a "new era" with a breed of neo-dinosaurs called family systems.

The more insightful reader will readily see that I agree with what Don Jackson meant. I just wish he had said what he meant. We all have a long way to go from there. Let's get on with it.

DON D. JACKSON

Dr. Vassiliou's remarks are penetrating and his admonitions are well taken. In fact, I can find nothing to disagree with in his comments and am glad, for this reason, that I hope to study at his institute next year.

I quite agree also with Dr. Epstein's admonitions and add another point to the "pitchman" characteristic that he so correctly puts his finger on. That is, it is quite possible that pitchmen are reacted to, in part, because of fear of changing the status quo. Those of us who have spent many thousands of hours and thousands of dollars learning to become psychoanalysts have a real investment in not throwing this particular baby out with any bath water. Yet I suspect this bias will in the long run prove to be costly to us and will take a lot of "pitching" to radically alter the thinking of the middle aged and older generations. This brings me to Dr. Lyman Wynne's comments. He also suggests that I have created too much of an either/or position and would substitute the idea of open link systems in which two of the systems that can be linked are individual personality and family systems. Again, that sounds very good and like peace in the world and motherhood, I'm all for it; yet I wonder if "open linked systems" isn't also an attempt to save psychoanalytic tenets which have grown rusty and reified over the years.

Finally, it is entirely possible to agree with Dr. Wynne's final comments, "Let's get on with it." There is a great deal to be done, but according to the philosopher of science, Kuhn, all significant scientific advances have been breakthroughs. If this is true, we won't get on with it by hard work alone but by having new ideas—at whatever cost to the old.

NOTES

1. G. Vassiliou, "Aspects of Parent-Adolescent Transaction in the Greek Family," in *The Adolescent in a Changing World*. Kaplan and Lebovici (Eds.), Basic Books. In print.
2. G. Vassiliou, Formal Discussion of Roy R. Grinker's Sr. paper, "Normality. Viewed as a System," General Systems Theory Session, APA Meeting, Detroit, May 8–12, 1967.
3. Harry Triandis, V. Vassiliou, and M. Nassiakou, "Some Cross-Cultural Studies of Subjective Culture." *Technical Report No.* 45 Urbana: Group Effectiveness Lab., 1967.

8

Family Interaction Patterns, Drug Treatment, and Change in Social Aggression

MELVIN COHEN
NORBERT FREEDMAN
DAVID M. ENGELHARDT
REUBEN A. MARGOLIS

Psychiatric literature is abundant with studies reporting the effectiveness of phenothiazine treatment in altering the behavior of mentally ill patients. When such studies are conducted within hospital or laboratory settings they are performed under relatively controlled environmental conditions which are usually conducive to behavioral change among patients. However, when studying the effects of treatment among a population of clinic patients, those who are living at home while receiving medication, the environment in which the anticipated behavioral change is expected to occur may differ according to variability in family culture. The basic assumption underlying this paper is that the families of psychiatric patients can be differentiated according to modal patterns of social interaction between family members and that different interactional patterns will modify the effects of phenothiazine treat-

From *Archives of General Psychiatry*, Vol. 19, July 1958, pp. 50–56. This study was supported by grants from the National Institute of Mental Health, Public Health Service (MH 01983 and MH 05090).

ment. The specific behavior studied was the alteration of social aggression among a sample of chronic schizophrenic outpatients receiving either chlorpromazine, promazine, or placebo treatment.

The reduction of aggressive behavior with drug therapy, especially phenothiazine treatment, has been widely reported in the literature.[1-3] Most of the studies reported have dealt primarily with hospitalized psychiatric patients or experimental subjects studied in a controlled laboratory setting. In the present study, we are concerned with the way social milieu mediates the phenothiazine treatment of aggressive behavior among schizophrenic outpatients. In reviewing social and psychological factors affecting drug treatment, Honigfeld[4] stresses the importance of taking into consideration the milieu or social environment in which the drug is administered. For example, in studying hospitalized psychiatric patients, the social environment in which treatment is given is usually positively oriented; the patient is encouraged to modify his aggressive and other "symptomatic" behavior. On the other hand, there may be an environmental "antidrug" effect,[5] i.e., the context in which medication is given may work against the potentially beneficial effects of a drug.

Families of psychiatric patients attending a large community outpatient clinic are quite heterogeneous in their social and psychological structure and thus may have varying impacts on the modification of patient behavior. In studying various aspects of the family functioning of psychiatric out-patients, it would be desirable to more fully understand the effects of the social environment on drug effectiveness. The problem, therefore, becomes one of differentiating families on the basis of those variables which would lead to the prediction of differential effects of phenothiazine treatment on aggressive behavior.

The relationship between the family unit as a closed social system and drug effectiveness has been discussed by Lennard.[6] Basically, a social system may be defined as one in which members show some responsiveness towards each other, some awareness of each other's actions and reactions, and maintain some level of affective input. Systems make different demands upon their members according to both the *degree* (greater or lesser), and *type* (positive or negative) of intrasystem inputs required. Therefore, according to Lennard the differential demand for affective input in diverse family systems should be reflected in the effects of drug treatment on affective behavior.

The variable which we have chosen as a measure of the level of negative affective input required in a family system is the degree of conflict and tension which is characteristic of the interrelationships between the patient and other family members. The measure of conflict and tension in the home is not viewed as indicating a temporary crisis situation, but rather as a reflection of a predominant mode of interaction among the family members.

A family unit characterized by a high degree of conflict and tension requires a greater amount of aggressively oriented behavior from its members than one which is low in conflict and tension. In a high conflict and tension family, not only is there a higher tolerance of aggressive behavior, but such behavior is the expected mode of social interaction. Thus, the effects of a purportedly aggression-reducing drug, such as chlorpromazine, should be minimized when administered within the context of an aggression-demanding environment (high conflict and tension). The same drug administered within a family system which required less aggressively oriented behavior from its members (low conflict and tension) should prove more effective in the reduction of such behavior.

Method

Subjects. The subjects were 54 male and 72 female psychiatric patients selected from a population of over 500 patients attending a community outpatient clinic utilizing psychotropic agents. The sample of 126 patients consisted of those patients who had obtained high intake scores on a measure of social aggression at home, and who had remained in treatment for at least three months. All patients had received a primary diagnosis of schizophrenic reaction with evidence of schizophrenic symptoms of at least one year's duration. The age range was 18 to 42 years.

Treatment Procedure

Using a double-blind procedure, patients were randomly assigned to one of three drug treatments; chlorpromazine, promazine, or placebo. The patient also received supportive therapy from the psychiatrist. The double-blind drug administration was maintained with provisions for flexible dosage administration. Mean daily dosage level for patients on active drug was approximately 180 mg with a range from 100 to 400 mg. Several checks were employed to ascertain that patients were in fact taking their medication as prescribed (reports by the patient and family members, periodic urine examinations, etc). Patients were seen weekly for the first month of treatment and biweekly thereafter.

Social Behavior Interview

A close relative of the patient was interviewed at intake and at the end of three months. The interviewer, using an open-ended questionnaire, attempted to ascertain from the relative the patient's behavior at home and in the community as perceived by that relative. We specifically used open-ended questions so that the relative could give us any information which he felt was relevant, without being restricted as to specific behaviors on the part of the patient. The interviews were coded independently of the interviewer, and the patient was given scores on the various items. The measures of conflict, tension, and social aggression were derived from the information given by the relative.

Measure of Conflict and Tension in the Home

The measure of conflict and tension in the home was derived from the intake interview with the relative. The items comprising this measure are concerned with the amount and locus of stress in the relationship between the patient and significant others, (e.g., parent, sibling, or spouse) and therefore, refer to relatively stable and habitual modes of behavior within the family unit. They measure the need within the family system for negative affective input. One end of the scale represents a low need for stressful input, as reflected in ratings indicating either complete absence of tension or tension not attributed to significant others; the other end of the scale indicates the presence of a high degree of tension within the family unit.

The four items derived from the relative's response which comprise the conflict and tension scale are:

1. *The person whom the patient likes the most.* A low score represents that the patient likes everyone and gets along well with everyone at home; a high score indicates that the patient does not get along with anyone or the liked person is out of the home.

2. *What characteristic of the patient does the relative most like.* A low score represents the frequent occurrence of some liked behavior; a high score indicates that the liked behavior occurs rarely or never.

3. *The person whom the patient dislikes the most.* A low score indicates that the patient gets along with everyone or the person the patient dislikes does not live with the patient; a high score means that the disliked person is someone who lives with the patient.

4. *What the patient does to give the relative a "hard time" (something which the relative perceives as negative).* A low score represents a minor complaint involving, in the relative's estimate, trivial "misbehavior"; a high score represents a strong complaint about what the relative perceives as highly negative behavior.

The scores for each item were equally weighted and summed to give one score as a measure of conflict and tension in the home. The range of scores was from 0 to 8. The correlation between baseline and three month scores for the clinic population was 0.65 (r_{tet}, $P < 0.001$), indicating that this is a reliable measure of the degree of conflict and tension in the home.

Measure of Social Aggression

A series of social traits was derived from the information given by the relative in the interview. These traits were considered as representing the relative's perceptions of the type of interpersonal behavior manifested by the patient in the home. The derivation of these traits and more specifically, how they were scored, is presented in detail in another paper.[7] The following social traits were scored: solitariness, implicit opposition, explicit opposition, ineffectual behavior, sickness, and responsible behavior. The subject's score represented the arcsine transformation of the percentage of units given by the relative in terms of each specific social trait. Thus, a patient could have high scores on several traits and low scores on the others, or an extremely high score on one trait, and relatively low scores on the remaining traits.

Explicit opposition (EO) is used as a measure of the patient's social aggressiveness at home. The trait is operationally defined as any report by the relative that the patient has been speaking or acting abusively or violently in the home. Examples of such socially aggressive behavior would be: "She screamed at me all morning"; "He woke up angry—everything made him jump at you"; "He hits the children for no reason at all." The patient population chosen for this study were those exhibiting high social aggression, i.e., those whose intake score on EO was 20.0 or above (somewhat above the median 18.4 for the entire clinic population). Change in social aggression was measured after three months of treatment.

Description of High Social Aggression Sample

In order to more fully understand this particular sample as distinct from the remainder of our patient population, a series of correlations of the EO scores with a host of other variables was performed for the total clinic population. The results of the correlational analysis are presented in Table 1.

TABLE 1: *Correlates of Social Aggression (as Measured by the Social Trait Score of Explicit Oppositionalism):* $N = 500$

Variable	Pearsonian r*	Meaning of Finding for High Aggression Sample
Demographic		
Sex	0.12*	Predominantly female
Social Behavior		
Conflict and Tension	0.47†	Higher conflict and tension at home
Social Pathology	0.39†	Relative complains about patient's behavior
Solitariness	−0.31†	Relative perceives patient as being nonsolitary
Responsibleness	−0.31†	Relative perceives patient as low in responsible behavior
Psychological		
Rozenzweig Picture-Frustration Test	0.125*	Patient high in fantasy aggression
Manifest Anxiety Scale	0.13*	Patient high in anxiety
Guardedness	0.00	
Psychiatric		
Attitude toward Illness	0.12*	Patient concerned about illness
Affect Restraint	0.15*	Psychiatrist rates patient as emotionally hyperactive
Paranoid Thinking	0.03	—
Acting Out	0.075	—
Cooperativeness	−0.065	—
Psychotic Deviation Scale	−0.02	—
Activity	0.05	—

*P <0.01.
†P <0.001.

The analysis suggests that the socially aggressive patient, based on the EO score, is most likely to be a woman who is relatively high in anxiety, emotionally hyperactive, concerned about her illness, not socially isolated or solitary, and described by the relative as not showing much responsible behavior.

There is also a significant relationship between the amount of conflict and tension in the home and the patient's level of social aggression ($r = 0.47$). The more aggressive the patient, the greater the conflict and tension in the home. However, among our high aggression sample, we were able to dichotomize patients into two groups according to the level of conflict and tension in the home. This was done by ranking the patients in the high aggression sample on the measure of conflict and tension, and by using a median break, designating one half of the sample as coming from homes characterized as relatively low in conflict and tension and the other half as relatively high on this variable. (The median for the high aggression sample was 4.5 as compared with a median of 3.3 for the total patient population). The baseline scores in aggression were similar for the two conflict and tension groups (low = 26.4; high = 27.4, $t < 1.00$). Thus, we were able to study aggressive patients who were functioning within two different social milieu; one characterized by high conflict and tension and one in which there was low conflict and tension.

Of interest are also the variables which were *not* significantly related to social aggression. One would anticipate that a highly aggressive patient would be seen by the psychiatrist as highly paranoid and as showing much acting-out behavior. However, this was not the case. There is no significant relationship between the psychiatrist's evaluations of paranoid thinking and acting-out behavior and the measure of social aggression. In addition, the psychiatrist does not rate the socially aggressive patient as higher in severity of illness or as being less cooperative in the clinic. However, the aggressive patient does receive a high score on the Rozenzweig Picture-Frustration Test which was used to measure fantasy aggression.

The general lack of correlation between the relative's reports of the patient's aggressiveness at home and the psychiatrist's evaluations of the patient's behavior in treatment suggests that the aggressive behavior is specific to the home situation and may not be carried over to the patient's behavior in the clinic.

RESULTS

We have predicted that the characteristic patterns of interpersonal behavior between the patient and other family members will determine the effectiveness of specific drugs on modifying the patient's aggressive behavior after three months of treatment. The measure of conflict and tension in the home was chosen as a reflection of the patterns of family interaction. The results of the analysis of variance of change in social aggression by drug treatment and level of conflict and tension are presented in Table 2. There is a significant interaction between these two independent variables ($F=5.08$, df$=2/120$, $P<0.01$), indicating that the patient's response to drug was different within the two contrasting social situations. For the

TABLE 2: *Mean Change in Social Aggression after Three Months of Treatment: Conflict and Tension by Drug*

Conflict and Tension	N	Chlor-promazine *	N	Pro-mazine	N	Placebo
High	20	−5.67*	21	−7.48	21	−6.50
Low	22	−15.13*	21	−4.24	21	−5.36

Analysis of Variance†

Source	df	MS	F
Drug	2	13.54	2.97 ‡
Conflict and tension	1	4.31	—
Drug × conflict and tension	2	23.17	5.08§
Within	120	4.56	—

*Baseline scores in Social Aggression were not significantly different between these two groups (high, M = 26.4; low, M = 27.3).
†Unequal n design.[10]
‡$P<0.10$.
§$P<0.01$.

high conflict and tension sample, mean change in social aggression after three months of treatment is the same whether the patient received active drug (chlorpromazine, —5.67; promazine, —7.48, or placebo, —6.50). For the low conflict and tension sample, however, there is a significantly greater reduction in social aggression among those patients who had received chlorpromazine treatment (—15.13) than among those who had received either promazine (—4.24) or placebo (—5.36) treatment. In fact, a series of *t*-test analyses show that the reduction in social aggression or the chlorpromazine treated patients in the low conflict and tension conditions is not only significantly greater ($P<0.01$) than the decrease observed in the comparable promazine and placebo treated patients, but is also significantly greater than the reduction in social aggression observed in the chlorpromazine treated high conflict and tension group. Though there is a general decrease in socially aggressive behavior after three months of clinic attendance, a significantly larger decrease occurs among those patients who were being treated with chlorpromazine and living in a home characterized as low in conflict and tension.

Daily modal dosage of chlorpromazine prescribed for each patient was examined to exclude the possibility that differences in reduction of aggression were merely reflections of differences in drug dosage between the low and high conflict and tension samples. It was found that the average daily dosage was 185 mg for the low conflict and tension sample and 213 mg for the high conflict and tension sample. This difference (which was in the opposite direction) was *not* statistically significant ($t<1.00$).

We now wish to consider whether this change in aggression as reported by a relative of the patient is manifested by other measures involving aggressive behavior or thought. The chlorpromazine treated low and high conflict and tension groups were compared with each other for possible change in either the psychological or psychiatric variables related to aggressiveness. Table 3 presents the mean change scores for each group.

TABLE 3: *Three Month Change Scores in Related Measures of Aggressiveness: Low vs High Conflict and Tension Groups (Chlorpromazine Treated Patients Only)*

Variable	Conflict and Tension		Range of Change Scores	t-test	P
	High (N = 20)	Low (N = 22)			
Picture-Frustration Test	+0.75	+1.24	−2.00 to +5.00	<1.00	N.S.
Guardedness	−0.25	−0.24	−2.00 to +2.00	<1.00	N.S.
Acting Out	−0.09	−0.18	−1.00 to +0.50	<1.00	N.S.
Cooperativeness	−0.09	+0.03	−1.17 to +0.84	<1.00	N.S.
Paranoid Thinking	−0.06	−0.38	−1.50 to +0.80	<1.80	.10
Affect Restraint*	−0.11	−0.02	−1.20 to +1.50	<1.00	N.S.
Manifest Anxiety Scale	−0.44	−0.82	−10.00 to +7.00	<1.00	N.S.

* A decrease indicates a lessening of emotional hyperactivity.

Seven variables were tested: (1) the Rozenzweig Picture-Frustration Test which was used to measure fantasy aggression; (2) patient's scores on the Manifest Anxiety Scale (MAS); (3) a Measure of Guardedness which was derived from the patient's *type* of responses to the Rorschach, the MAS and the F-Scale; (4) the psychiatrist's evaluations of Acting Out behavior; (5) degree of Affect Restraint; (6) cooperativeness in the clinic; and (7) level of Paranoid Thinking.

An analysis of Table 3 indicates that none of these variables differentiated the high from the low conflict and tension groups. The difference in Paranoid Thinking came the closest to being statistically significant, but missed the 0.05 level of significance. Nonetheless, many of the differences were in the expected direction; the low conflict and tension patients decreased in their acting-out behavior, received lower scores on the MAS, became less paranoid, and were seen as being more cooperative in the clinic. However, as none of these differences reached significance, we have to conclude that the decrease in social aggression as reported by a relative of the patient, is *not* reflected in any other measures of aggressive or oppositional behavior.

COMMENT

In this paper we have attempted to demonstrate that the social milieu in which a psychotropic agent is administered must be taken into account in studying the effectiveness of the agent in modifying behavior. Our particular emphasis has been on the reduction of aggressive behavior with chlorpromazine treatment among a population of chronic schizophrenic outpatients. We found that in homes characterized as high in conflict and tension, in which aggressively oriented behavior is a predominant and apparently a neccessary mode of adaptation, the aggressive patient who receives chlorpromazine does *not* show a significant reduction in aggressive behavior; whereas in a home characterized as low in conflict and tension, in which aggressively oriented behavior is *not* the predominant and apparently necessary mode of social adaptation, aggressive patients who are treated with chlorpromazine *do* show a significant reduction in aggressive behavior.

In the low conflict and tension home the patient's aggressiveness is dissonant with the general pattern of interaction among the family members. The home may be characterized as comparatively harmonious and tranquil. The relative perceives everyone as "getting along" with each other. There is a minimum amount of overt friction in the every-day interactional behaviors. It is possible, of course, that there is much denial and inhibition of aggressively oriented behavior—but the overt patterns of behavior are suggestive of a relatively tranquil and placid home environment. In this type of home environment, chlorpromazine, by reducing the patient's aggressiveness, reduces the dissonance between the patient's behavior and the predominant mode of social adaptation of the family unit.

The high conflict and tension home, on the other hand, is characterized by a great amount of aggressively-oriented behavior such as continual and persistent shouting and yelling in which the family members are constantly provoking each other. Each person's behavior is a stimulus for aggression in the others. In this type of social situation a reduction in social aggression by chlorpromazine would increase the dissonance between the patient's behavior and the predominant mode of social adaptation and the family would become more provocative of aggressive behavior in the patient in order to reduce the dissonance within the social unit.

The family mode of social adaptation may be seen in terms of a homeostatic balance which is upset by the reduction in the patient's aggression. Jackson[8] discusses the concept of "family homeostasis" in terms of communication theory; family interaction is depicted as a closed information system in which variation in output or behavior are fed back in order to correct the system's response. Therefore, in order to restore the balance, the patient's relatives should increase their role as aggression-inducing stimuli until the balance is restored and the patient's level of aggressiveness again fits into the family pattern.

A similar model of family behavior is proposed by Haley in terms of a self-corrective governed system.

> If a family confines itself to repetitive patterns within a certain range of possible behavior, then they are confined to that range by some sort of governing process. No outside governor requires the family members to behave in their habitual patterns, so this governing process must exist within the family. . . . To describe families, the most appropriate analogy would seem to be the self-corrective system governed by family members influencing each other's behavior and thereby establishing rules and prohibitions for that particular family system. Such a system tends to be error-activated. Should other family members break a family rule, the others become activated until he either conforms to the rule again or successfully establishes a new one (p. 373).[9]

The model of a homeostatic balance as explaining the findings of the present study requires further support. We have not directly observed the patient's behavior in the family unit but have had to rely on an analysis of a report of it from a family member. Secondly, in this discussion we have employed the simplifying assumption that the measured mode of family adaptation characterizes all members of the family. It may well be that the predominant mode of family adaptation may vary as a function of the particular subunits of a family that is studied.[10]

The foregoing discussion is of special relevance when we consider the problem of therapeutic intervention in the situation where the patient lives in a family characterized by a high demand for aggressive behavior. Ideally, one may attempt to separate the patient from the family unit or help him to participate in the family pattern at minimal personal cost. Such solutions are difficult to achieve in chronic schizophrenic outpatients under a regimen of psychotropic agents and brief supportive psychotherapy.

A more feasible strategy may be family therapy. If all the family members can be involved in the problem of modifying interactional patterns they may draw support from each other in this difficult task. Alteration of the family pattern to some degree may well alter the effectiveness of psychotropic agents on patients residing in such units. The degree of change necessary remains to be determined. One must also consider the possibility that this kind of social aggression which is generally viewed as symptomatic behavior may not at all be what brought this type of patient into treatment. Although the behavior is obvious and generally socially disapproved, the patient and his family may want help with other problems.

Conclusion

Chronic schizoprenic patients attending a community clinic were randomly assigned to one of three treatment conditions; chlorpromazine, promazine, or placebo and studied for change in aggressive behavior after three months of treatment. It was predicted that the degree of conflict and tension characterizing the patient's home milieu would be a factor in modifying the potential effectiveness of drug treatment on aggressive behavior. The results show that the most significant decrease in aggression occurred among the chlorpromazine treated patients from low conflict and tension homes. The decrease for chlorpromazine treated patients from high conflict and tension homes was the same as that for promazine and placebo treated patients, regardless of degree of conflict and tension. The results were interpreted as indicating that chlorpromazine will significantly reduce a patient's aggressive behavior if that behavior is dissonant with family interactional patterns (low conflict and tension) and will be less effective in those situations in which aggressive behavior is consistent with family interactional patterns (high conflict and tension).

REFERENCES

1. Casey, J. F., et al. Treatment of Schizophrenic Reactions With Phenothiazine Derivatives. *Amer. J. Psychiat.*, *117*:97–105, August 1960.
2. Cole, H. F., and H. H. Wolf. The Effects of Some Psychotropic Drugs on Conditioned Avoidance and Aggressive Behaviors. *Psychopharmacologia,8*:389–396, 1966.
3. Klein, D. F., and M. Fink. Behavioral Reaction Patterns With Phenothiazines. *Arch. Gen. Psychiat.*, *7*:447–459, December 1962.
4. Honigfeld, G. Non-Specific Factors in Treatment: II. Review of Social Psychological Factors. *Dis. Nerv. Syst., 25*:225–239, April 1964.
5. Knobel, M. The Environmental Anti-Drug Effect. *Psychiatry,* *23*:403–407, November 1960.
6. Lennard, H. L. A Proposed Program of Research in Sociopharmacology. Symposium presentation on "Psychological Approaches to Social Behavior" at the Harvard Medical School, April 1963.
7. Mann, D., et al. A Method for Measuring Social Behavior of Psychiatric Outpatients. *Psychol. Rep.*, *18*:371–378, April 1966.
8. Jackson, D. D. The Question of Family Homeostasis. *Psychiat. Quart. Suppl., 31*:79–90, 1957.
9. Haley, J. The Family of the Schizophrenic: A Model System. *J. Nerv. Ment. Dis.*, *129*:357–374, October 1959.
10. Walker, H. M., and J. Lev. *Statistical Inference.* New York: Holt, Rinehart and Winston, Inc., 1953, pp. 381–382.

9

Interaction Patterns of Parents and Hospitalized Sons Diagnosed as Schizophrenic or Nonschizophrenic

AMERIGO FARINA
JULES D. HOLZBERG

The present study, in general, attempts to clarify the role of the family in schizophrenia. Specifically, it is concerned with two kinds of behaviors which theory and past research suggest merit particular attention in the attempt to assess the role of the family in this condition. These are dominating and conflictful or hostile behavior. Some of the relevant studies will briefly be reviewed.

There are a rather large number of reports which indicate that schizophrenic patients emerge from families characterized by atypical dominance patterns (Farina, 1960; Farina and Dunham, 1963; Kohn and Clausen, 1956; Lidz, Cornelison, Fleck, and Terry, 1957a; Reichard and Tillman, 1950). These studies consistently suggest that one of the parents is unduly

From *Journal of Abnormal Psychology*, Vol. 73, No. 2, 1968, pp. 114–118. Copyright 1968 by the American Psychological Association. This study was financed by a research grant from the National Institute of Mental Health, United States Public Health Service (M-6167).

dominating over the other, although Caputo (1963) reports finding no differences of this kind between parents of nonhospitalized male veterans and parents of male schizophrenic Ss. In some studies (Farina, 1960; Farina and Dunham, 1963), the parents of the schizophrenic patients have been divided into two groups on the basis of the offspring's premorbid adjustment as measured by the Phillips (1953) scale.[1] The dominance relationships were found to differ between these two classes of parents. In the case of parents whose sons' premorbid adjustment was reasonably adequate (Goods), the fathers were more dominant than their wives, whereas women whose sons' adjustment had been marginal (Poors) were more assertive than their husbands. The Farina and Dunham study suggested, in addition, that when sons are included as members of the interacting family group, Goods are more assertive and dominant vis-à-vis their parents than are Poors.

Studies which have measured conflictful and hostile behavior have typically reported that it is present in greater degree in families of schizophrenic than in families of control Ss (Caputo, 1963; Farina, 1960; Farina and Dunham, 1963; Fisher, Boyd, Walker, and Sheer, 1959; Lidz, Cornelison, Fleck, and Terry, 1957b). As with dominance, when the parents of Goods are compared with the parents of Poors, differences between them are found indicating that conflict is particularly intense in the Poor families (Farina, 1960; Farina and Dunham, 1963). Including the son in the interaction reveals some additional and quite suggestive differences between Good and Poor families in the way they express hostility. Not only did the Poor families diplay more conflict but a considerably greater *proportion* of it was directed from one parent to the other, suggesting that these parents are impatient with each other and hold each other in poor regard (Farina and Dunham, 1963). On the other hand, Good parents seemed more tolerant and respectful of each other. They could agree with each other when the son, unlike the Poor son, expressed views different from theirs and maintained these views in the face of parental opposition.

The present study, then, follows this line of research into the characteristics of families of schizophrenic patients.

METHOD

The Ss of this study were three groups of hospitalized male psychiatric patients and the patients' biological parents. These Ss are described in detail in a report of other findings (Farina and Holzberg, 1967). All had to meet a number of rather stringent criteria. One group ($N=24$) consisted of nonschizophrenic psychiatric patients, while all patients in the remaining two groups were diagnosed as schizophrenic, one group ($N=26$) being composed of patients rated as Goods while patients in the last group ($N=24$) were classed as Poors.

The procedure used is also fully described in the earlier report. In brief, the mother, son, and father were individually asked to tell how they believed six hypothetical problem situations involving parents and children should be resolved.[2] The three members were then brought together and asked to indicate how they would resolve the same problems as a family. Both the individual and joint sessions were tape-recorded, and the recordings were subsequently used to obtain measures of dominating and conflictful behavior.

The four dominance indexes used, together with the reliability of each, are also described in the report by Farina and Holzberg (1967). Of course, in addition to scoring the parental behaviors, the dominating behavior displayed by the son was also scored in the present study. Hence, some additional information regarding how reliably this behavior could be scored is required. For the index *Total time spoken*, the interrater correlation for the son was .93 and for *Total yielding* it was .78.

The conflict indexes, which were derived entirely from the group recordings, are not described in the earlier study. They were selected with the aim of having them reflect the lack of respect and intolerance the family members felt toward each other as well as to indicate the extent to which they could compromise and cooperate. The indexes used and the reliability of each were as follows:

1. Frequency of simultaneous speech. The number of times in the interview during which two, or all three, members spoke

concurrently. Larger scores are assumed to reflect greater degrees of conflict present. The interrater correlation for each family member was above .90 and for total simultaneous speech occurring within the family it was .99.

2. Failure to reach agreement. The number of hypothetical problems for which the family members failed to arrive at a mutually satisfactory solution. The raters agreed as to whether it had occurred or not on 73 of 78 possibilities for 94% agreement. Where each had scored a disagreement (39 situations), there was exact agreement between the raters as to which members disagreed with which others for 90% of the occurrences.

3. Interruptions. The number of times during the interview that a family member interrupted another. The interrater agreement for total interruptions occurring within the family was .97. The agreement as to which member interrupted which other ranged from a low of .59 for fathers interrupting the son to a high of 1.00 for sons interrupting the father.

4. Disagreements and aggressions. The number of times one of the family members disagreed with or displayed aggressive behavior toward another. The interrater agreement for total number of disagreements and aggressions occurring within a family was .86. The agreement as to which member disagreed with or was aggressive toward which other ranged from a low of .49 for mothers displaying such behavior toward the son, to a high of .96 for mothers behaving in this way toward the father.

In rating those tape recordings for dominance and conflict behaviors, the judges[3] were kept entirely ignorant of the group membership of the families they were rating. This procedure makes it highly unlikely that any systematic bias crept into the scores assigned these families.

RESULTS

The mean dominance scores obtained by the three groups of families are presented in Table 1. In interpreting these scores,

TABLE 1: *Mean Dominance Scores for Families of Control, Good and Poor Subjects*

	No. times spoken[a]	Total times spoken[a]	Passive acceptance[b]	Total yielding[b]
Controls (N = 24)				
Mother	6.3	289	.6	1.7
Son	4.7	252	.7	1.1
Father	7.2	348	.2	1.1
Goods (N = 26)				
Mother	7.1	301	.2	1.5
Son	4.2	259	.6	1.9
Father	6.3	350	.2	.8
Poors (N = 24)				
Mother	4.0	336	.1	.8
Son	4.0	213	1.0	2.1
Father	7.1	422	.4	.8

[a] High score = high dominance.
[b] Low score = high dominance.

it must be remembered that for *Passive acceptance* and *Total yielding,* in contrast to the other two indexes, a low score signifies high dominance. The most obvious pattern apparent in this table is that each index shows the Poor sons to be less dominant than sons in either of the other two groups. Some of the indexes suggest the Poor mothers are more dominant than mothers in the other two groups but the trend is not particularly convincing.

The scores of each index for each family member were individually analyzed using a Kruskal-Wallis test (Siegel, 1956). This is a nonparametric technique suitable for determining if a series of independent samples are drawn from different populations. These analyses revealed that only for the yielding scores of the sons did these groups reach a statistically significant level ($p < .05$).

Mann-Whitney U tests were subsequently used to determine which two groups of sons were significantly different from each other. These tests indicated that Poor sons had significantly higher total yielding scores than sons in the Control group ($z=2.38$, $p<.05$), suggesting that the former group of patients is less assertive than the latter. No other statistically significant differences were found for the dominance scores.

The conflict scores received by Ss are shown in Table 2. The table shows not only the total conflict displayed by the families for each of the indexes, but also provides specific information as to which members were experiencing conflict with which others. For example, one can tell that for Control families there were, on the average, 23.4 instances of simultaneous speech during the group resolution of the hypothetical problems and of this total an average of 9.3 involved the mother and father. The table reveals several consistent patterns. The totals for each index are highest for the families of the schizophrenic patients, suggesting that these families experience greater conflict in their interactions than the Control families. An examination of the specific locus of the conflict within the families also reveals a highly consistent and interesting pattern. Six of the seven indexes which reflect conflict between the mother and father, even though the son may have been involved, indicate the Control parents experience the least, Goods are intermediate, and Poor parents experience the most conflict. The exception is the index *Father interrupts Mother* for which the order of the Goods and Poors is reversed but even for this index the least conflict is shown by the Control parents. Thus, there is a trend suggesting that parents of schizophrenic patients experience greater conflict in their interaction than parents of Controls and that this conflict is particularly intense for parents of Poors.

Kruskal-Wallis tests were used to determine if the three groups differed for any of the indexes shown in Table 2. While the groups approached being significantly different for several of the indexes, for none were they clearly different at the .05 level of probability. In view of the fact that prior research using the Phillips scale has consistently revealed that patients

TABLE 2: *Mean Conflict Scores for Families of Control, Good, and Poor Subjects*

	Controls	Goods	Poors
Frequency of simultaneous speech			
Total	23.4	31.1	24.8
Mo, Fa	9.3	13.5	15.2
Mo, Son	7.2	9.3	5.1
Fa, Son	5.7	6.3	3.9
Mo, Fa, Son	1.2	2.1	.5
Failure to reach agreement			
Total	2.4	3.0	3.4
Mo vs Son, Fa	.4	.69	.75
Son vs Mo, Fa	.7	1.0	1.2
Fa vs Mo, Son	.7	.9	1.0
Fa vs Mo vs Son	.6	.4	.4
Interruptions			
Total	5.8	8.7	6.8
Mo intrp Fa	1.2	2.1	3.0
Mo intrp Son	1.5	.8	.9
Fa intrp Mo	1.1	2.0	1.5
Fa intrp Son	.6	1.3	.6
Son intrp Mo	.9	1.8	.5
Son intrp Fa	.6	.8	.3
Disagreements and aggressions			
Total	15.3	19.2	15.5
Mo ag Fa	2.7	3.0	3.5
Mo ag Son	2.6	3.4	2.0
Fa ag Mo	1.9	2.7	3.0
Fa ag Son	2.4	2.8	2.5
Son ag Mo	2.6	4.0	1.7
Son ag Fa	3.1	3.3	2.7

Note. Key to abbreviations used: Mo = mother; Fa = father; vs = against; intrp = interrupts; ag = disagrees or aggresses toward.

and parents falling in the Poor group are most deviant in comparison to Control groups while Goods are intermediate, a series of analyses was done to determine if the Poor and Control groups differed. Mann-Whitney U tests revealed a number of significant differences between these two groups.

The Poor families experienced significantly more total *Failures to reach agreement* than Controls ($z=2.01$, $p<.05$). Also, for those *Failures to reach agreement* which were due to conflict between the parents (Mother against Son, Father plus Father against Mother, Son), the Poor families were significantly higher than the latter group ($z=2.00$, $p<.05$). Quite consistent with this result, Poor families are significantly higher ($z=2.25$, $p<.05$) than Controls for number of *Disagreements and aggressions* reflecting paternal disagreement with the mother (Father aggresses toward Mother) and approach this level ($z=1.78$, $p<.10$) for the sum of these indexes which reflect parental strife (Mother aggresses toward Father plus Father aggresses toward Mother). There were no other significant differences between these groups nor were any found between Controls and Goods or Goods and Poors.

DISCUSSION

The results showing that Poor patients are less dominant than Control patients are consistent with a trend reported by Farina and Dunham (1963) who carried out a study very similar to the present one. Farina and Dunham had no control group but, as in the present study, Poors were found to be less assertive than Goods. The interesting question of whether the Poors are more passive than other psychiatric patients because it is the parents with whom they are interacting cannot be answered without additional research. Except for these results, the dominance findings are inconsistent with the rather large number of studies which were cited. These reports indicate that parents of schizophrenic patients relate to each other in aberrant ways as far as dominance is concerned, whereas in the present study no such behaviors were observed. This apparent discrepancy may be due to the many differences between the present and earlier studies, an important one being that in the present study dominance was measured behaviorally rather than in terms of a verbal report as is the more typical practice.

Also, in earlier investigations the control groups used have differed from the experimental group in many ways in addition to the diagnosis of schizophrenia. In this study, however, the control group Ss were well matched to the experimental groups in all seemingly relevant ways except for diagnosis. Moreover, other investigations of similar samples have failed to find dominance differences while finding differences in conflict as in the present study (Caputo, 1963). It would appear, therefore, that there are no differences with respect to dominance relationships between parents of schizophrenic patients and parents of other psychiatric patients or between parents of good and parents of poor premorbid schizophrenic patients.

Unlike dominance, the conflict findings are generally quite consistent with preceding research. As in previous studies, conflict was found to be higher for families of schizophrenics than for families of Controls although the Good-Poor differences as reported by Farina and Dunham (1963) were not found. Also, what seems to us particularly intriguing, the biggest group differences were found for conflict occurring *between parents* of schizophrenic patients while degree of parentson conflict did not seem particularly different across the groups. An implication of this result is that we should perhaps direct more attention to interparental relationships per se in trying to understand the genesis of schizophrenia. The correlation between degree of parental strife and severity of pathology on the part of the son supports this implication and is very consistent with contemporary psychogenic theories of schizophrenia which assign an important role to the family. The Poors, who have been shown to be more disturbed and less likely to recover than the Goods (Garmezy and Rodnick, 1959), have parents who display the most conflict, the parents of Goods are intermediate, and Controls, whose diagnoses indicate a less severe pathology, have parents who interact with the least friction of the three groups. Prior relevant studies are quite consistent with the present results (Farina, 1960; Farina and Dunham, 1963).

NOTES

1. For a review of research making use of the Phillips scale, see Herron (1962) and Garmezy and Rodnick (1959).
2. These situations are given in the earlier report (Farina and Holzberg, 1967).
3. Appreciation is expressed to Ross Hartsough and Douglas Kimura who did this demanding work.

REFERENCES

Caputo, D. V. The parents of the schizophrenic. *Family Process,* 1963, *2,* 339–356.

Farina, A. Patterns of role dominance and conflict in parents of schizophrenic patients. *Journal of Abnormal and Social Psychology,* 1960 *61,* 31–38.

Farina, A., and Dunham, R. M. Measurement of family relationships and their effects. *Archives of General Psychiatry,* 1963, *9,* 64–73.

Farina, A., and Holzberg, J. D. Attitudes and behaviors of fathers and mothers of male schizophrenic patients. *Journal of Abnormal Psychology,* 1967, *72,* 381–387.

Fisher, S., Boyd, I., Walker, D., and Sheer, D. Parents of schizophrenics, neurotics, and normals. *Archives of General Psychiatry,* 1959, *1,* 149–166.

Garmezy, N., Farina, A., and Rodnick, E. H. The structured situational test: A method for studying family interaction in schizophrenia. *American Journal of Orthopsychiatry,* 1960, *30,* 445–452.

Garmezy, N., and Rodnick, E. H. Premorbid adjustment and performance in schizophrenia: Implications for interpreting heterogeneity in schizophrenia. *Journal of Nervous and Mental Disease,* 1959, *129,* 450–466.

Herron, W. G. The process-reactive classification of schizophrenia. *Psychological Bulletin,* 1962, *59,* 329–343.

Kohn, M. L., and Clausen, J. A. Parental authority behavior and schizophrenia. *American Journal of Orthopsychiatry,* 1956, *26,* 297–313.

Lidz, T., Cornelison, A. R., Fleck, S., and Terry, D. The intrafamilial environment of the schizophrenic patient. *Psychiatry,* 1957, *20,* 329–342. (a)

Lidz, T., Cornelison, A. R., Fleck, S., and Terry, D. The intrafamilial environment of schizophrenic patients: II. Marital schism and marital skew. *American Journal of Psychiatry,* 1957, *144,* 241–248. (b)

Phillips, L. Case history data and prognosis in schizophrenia. *Journal of Nervous and Mental Disease,* 1953, *117,* 515–525.

Reichard, S., and Tillman, C. Patterns of parent-child relationships in schizophrenia. *Psychiatry,* 1950, *13,* 247–257.

Siegel, S. *Nonparametric statistics.* New York: McGraw-Hill, 1956.

10 Interaction Testing in the Measurement of Marital Intelligence

GERALD BAUMAN
MELVIN ROMAN
JOSEPH BORELLO
BETTY MELTZER

The work reported here is the first step in an effort to develop a reliable and empirically valid method for studying the characteristics of families as interacting units. An increasing literature (e.g., Jackson and Satir, 1961) emphasizes the critical need for a technique for family diagnosis. While a variety of techniques exist for the evaluation of the individual family member, there are practically no such tools when it comes to making meaningful assessments of the family group as a psychosocial entity in itself. As a first consideration, therefore, a method was sought which would simultaneously provide meaningful information about individual members as well as information about the family as a social system.

From *Journal of Abnormal Psychology,* Vol. 72, No. 6, December 1967, pp. 489–495. Copyright 1967 by the American Psychological Association.

This research was supported by the following grants from the National Institute of Mental Health: No. 1-R11 MH-01132-01, S-R11 MH-01132-02, and S-R11 MH-91132-03.

If possible, such a method should also allow for the direct observation of behavior. Almost all of today's codified knowledge of families rests on studies using interview or questionnaire reports. While such data are of value, they are known to be subject to distortion both consciously and unconsciously. Data derived from clinical experience with families in therapy, while often provocative and stimulating, likewise suffer from serious methodological flaws. The subjective biases of therapists or observers are a continuously operating and inadequately evaluated factor. Thus, a method allowing direct observation of interaction is highly desirable.

A third consideration was that the data should be collected in a standardized manner, identical for all families, and repeatable.

Finally, a method was sought which would make the decision-making process and communication patterns readily available for analysis. Much recent literature suggests that decision-making processes may be a useful approach to the categorization of families. The works of Jackson (Jackson and Satir, 1961) and Wynne (Wynne and Singer, 1963) linking thought disturbance in the primary patient to forms of thinking and communicating in family transactions, as well as Lidz's (Lidz, Cornelison, Fleck, and Terry, 1958) work on the "transmission of irrationality," all point to the need for the systematic exploration of the family as a perceiving, interpreting, communicating, decision-making social system.

The present investigation attacked the problem by exploring the usefulness of an approach to married couples based on some of the traditional clinical approaches to individuals. Tentatively, an assumption was made of individual-group psychological isomorphism, that is, that significant similarities exist between groups and individuals. The task then became, in part, an exploration of the usefulness as well as the limits of validity of this general hypothesis. (For a discussion of the uses and limitations of analogy models, see Hoffman and Arsenian, 1965.)

Initially, traditional psychological tests like the Wechsler-Bellevue, Rorschach, TAT, Figure Drawing, and Szondi had been applied to groups and familes ranging from two to nine members in a procedure called Interaction Testing (Roman and Bauman, 1960). This accumulation of case-by-case experience was then extended by the present systematic investigation of Interaction Testing in a study of the intellectual functioning of 50 married couples. The study is designed to evaluate the feasibility of Interaction Testing, the reliability of Interaction Test scores, and the nature of the contribution of husband and wife to Interaction IQ.

GENERAL PROCEDURE

Here martial intelligence was defined as the ability of the couple to solve problems conjointly, specifically a set of problems drawn from an individual intelligence test.

Each member of the couple was tested individually in the standard manner with the Comprehension and Similarities subtests of the Wechsler-Bellevue Intelligence Scale from both Forms I and II, yielding a total of 44 items. The couple was then brought together and the same 44 items were readministered to them as a couple. Thus, three types of data were elicited:

1. The test protocols of individual members which were scored and interpreted in the standard manner (Wechsler, 1944, 1946).

2. The test protocol of the couple which was scored as though it had been obtained from an individual.

3. The interaction "process" which could be inferred from a comparison of the couple product with individual protocols.

Subjects

Fifty married couples served as Ss in this study. They represent a random selection from among the (married) patients admitted to the Westchester Square Day Hospital of Albert Einstein College of Medicine. They do not differ from the Day Hospital population as regards diagnosis, patient gender, or age. (Thus, one spouse of each couple was a patient.) Of the primary patients in the sample, 22 were husbands and 28 were wives. Of these 50 patients, 35 were diagnosed as having been psychotic on admission (17 males, 18 females) and 15 as nonpsychotic (5 males, 10 females), though all were, of course, acutely disturbed upon admission. The average of the patient-Ss was 41, and the range was 23–80. The patient-Ss thus appear to be a representative sample of Day Hospital patients who in turn were demonstrated by Zwerling and Wilder (1963) to have been a representative sample of inpatient admissions to Jacobi Hospital of the Bronx Municipal Hospital Center.

The choice of this sample was dictated not only by practical (availability) considerations, but also by clinical and theoretical interests. It was felt that this use of an abnormal sample, if it were to bias the findings at all, would be likely to bias them in the direction of unreliability. In any event, future normal samples could serve to check on such sample influences.

Testing Procedure

Each patient-spouse was tested individually, approximately 1 week after his or her admission to the Day Hospital. The nonpatient-spouse was then tested individually as soon after the patient's administration as could be arranged. (This varied from the same day to 2 days later.) Only one couple was found to be untestable. Immediately following the individual testing of the spouse, the same tests were readministered to the couple together. During this "Interaction Testing," the two members were seated at a table next to each other and facing the examiner. The test answer form and a pencil were placed before the couple who were told that one of them was to record the couple's answer. The choice of "recorder" was made by the couple. (This differed from the individual testing where the examiner acted as recorder.)

The first Similarities item was then administered to the couple who discussed the question and arrived at a response which they recorded. If the couple was unable to arrive at an answer after a "reasonable" length of time, a further 1-minute time limit was then imposed. If this limit was exceeded, the examiner proceeded to the next item and the score 0 for "no answer" was recorded. This happened rarely.

RESULTS

Four areas are considered: (1) test behavior of the couples, (2) reliability of Interaction IQ scores, (3) analysis of the nature of husband and wife contributions, and (4) interaction process analysis. ("Interaction" will be capitalized when it refers to Interaction Testing procedure or scores, but will not be capitalized when referring to statistical interaction or interaction process analysis.)

Test Behavior

Conjoint testing, that is, the 44 items being jointly answered, required about 1 hour for most couples, which was approximately twice as long as individual testing time. The maximum testing time for any couple in the sample was about 2 hr. Of the 50 couples, 34 answered all items, 9 pairs left 1 item unanswered, and the remaining 7 ranged in unanswered items from 3 to 15. In only one case was there resistance to the task resulting in discontinuance. In general, it appeared to be as acceptable a procedure as individual testing, and was effected without any special difficulty. The choice of recorder was typically made by the couple quickly and with little discussion. In only one case was there a splitting of the recorder task between the two members. Twenty-six husbands and 23 wives served as recorders. This was not a significant difference. Thirty recorders were patients as against 19 nonpatient recorders. Again, this was not a significant difference $(.10 < p < .20)$. However, it may suggest a trend in the direction of selecting the patient as opposed to the nonpatient as recorder.

Reliability of IQ Test Scores

Table 1 presents the prorated IQ scores obtained by 50 married couples and the same 100 spouses on Forms I and II of the Wechsler-Bellevue Intelligence Scale (Comprehension and Similarities subtests).

TABLE 1: *Wechsler-Bellevue Prorated IQ Scores of 50 Married Couples*

Subjects	N	Form I		Form II		Pearson r: Form I vs. II[a]
		M	SD	M	SD	
Husband IQ	50	105.0	12.85	101.5	12.30	.85
Wife IQ	50	97.0	13.69	93.0	11.11	.82
Patient IQ	50	99.9	13.95	95.7	11.50	.88
Nonpatient IQ	50	102.1	13.70	98.7	13.21	.83
Interaction IQ	50	104.6	12.15	102.5	8.78	.85
Potential IQ	50	115.9	12.46	113.1	10.45	.84

Note. Based on Comprehension and Similarities subtests.
[a]Corrected by Spearman-Brown formula.

The split-half reliability of Interaction IQ, .85, is high and of the same order of magnitude as individual IQ reliabilities.

The mean Interaction IQ (i.e., the mean IQ of 50 couples tested as couples) is at about the same level as mean husband IQ, and about 8 IQ points above that of the wives; both are significantly higher than the wife IQ ($p < .002$, .001 for Forms I and II, respectively). There was no significant difference between nonpatient and patient IQ.

The literature on group problem solving, that is, "together versus apart" comparisons (as well as retest effects), suggests that the performance of the group generally surpasses that of each individual alone (e.g., Faust, 1959; Lorge & Solomon, 1955; Marquart, 1955; Taylor, 1954). On this basis, one might expect that the Interaction IQ would have been higher than the higher individual's IQ. Because this was not true of this group, it seems reasonable to speculate that inefficient teamwork held down the Interaction IQ, and that this may be related to pathological or destructive interaction within the couples.

To measure the degree of this "inefficiency" of the couples, the best score that each couple could have obtained, had they pooled their individual resources by always selecting the better of the two responses made individually, was calculated. This yields the so-called Potential IQ, defined as the score the couple would have obtained had they made optimal selections of their individual responses on each item.

Average Potential IQ for the 50 couples was 116 on Form I and 113 on Form II, as compared with the obtained Interaction IQs of 105 and 102, respectively; the corrected split-half reliability for the Potential measure is .84 (Table 1).

On the average, then, these couples did not do materially better than the husbands did alone, but could have increased the Interaction IQ by about 10 points (or one sigma) had there been more judicious pooling of individual resources (i.e., always using the better of the two answers they gave individually). On both Forms I and II the differences between Potential and Interaction IQ were significant at the .001 level, so this sample of 50 couples failed to make optimum use of the resources of the individual members. This difference may be one useful method for explicitly measuring a kind of task efficiency (or inefficiency) in marital pairs.

Analysis of the Nature of Husband and Wife Contributions

It would be wrong to infer that the wives made little or no contribution to Interaction IQ, however. Table 2 shows that both husbands and wives contribute substantially to Interaction IQ ($r=.814$, .699, respectively). Because the husband-wife correlation ($r=.492$) is appreciably lower than either of the others, the likelihood is that husbands and wives contribute somewhat differently to the joint product. Although the table thus suggests that there is a significant pooling of husband and

TABLE 2: *Pearson Product-Moment Correlations and Multiple Correlation of Husband IQ, Wife IQ, Husband IQ × Wife IQ, and Interaction IQ Scores*

IQ Score	Husband IQ	Wife IQ	Husband IQ × Wife IQ[a]	Interaction IQ	Beta	Beta × $r_{int, IQ}$
Husband IQ	—	.492[b]	.841	.814	.570	.464
Wife IQ	.492[b]	—	.875	.699	.337	.236
Husband IQ × Wife IQ	.841	.875	—	.867	.093	.081

Note. For $N = 50$, $r_{.05} = .276$, $r_{.01} = .358$, $r_{.001} = .447$. Regression Equation: $.492_H{}^b + .319_W + .0014_{HW} + 7.27 = $ Interaction IQ. Multiple $R_{int \cdot H, W, HW} = .883$. Coefficient of Multiple Determination $R^2 = .780$.

[a]The product of husband and wife IQ was selected as a general form of nonadditive score combination. Its purpose was to test in the regression equation for the possibility of significant nonadditive (or "emergent") determination of Interaction IQ from individual IQ scores.

[b]The identity of this value (.492) with the correlation between husband and wife IQ is coincidental.

wife contributions, a question often raised in the literature is that of the model that best accounts for the pooling of group members' resources (Restle and Davis, 1963). In other words, are the contributions of husband and wife to Interaction IQ of a simple additive (or subtractive) nature, or is there some more complex interaction between husband and wife scores such as a multiplicative one?

To evaluate this, a multiple correlation was computed using Interaction IQ as the criterion, with the predictors the individual IQs of husband and of wife, for which an R of .88 was obtained. This value is quite close to the theoretically maximum correlation of .92 that could be produced by correlating a perfectly reliable predictor with Interaction IQ. This finding alone suggests that no significant Interaction IQ variance is determined by other than individual spousal scores in some additive function. Further evaluating this issue, the regression equation (Table 2) specifies the prediction of Interaction IQ, from husband and wife IQs. As the beta weights for husband and wife were both significantly different from zero, one can say that both husband and wife made significant contributions to Interaction IQ. Multiplying the beta weight of each sex variable by its correlation with the criterion (Interaction IQ) yields a reflection of the degree of unique contribution of each sex, as well as the common (multiplicative) contribution of husbands and wives (.46, .24, .08, respectively). Thus, the husbands' unique contribution to Interaction IQ accounts for 46% of the variance, the wives' unique contribution accounts for 24% of the variance, and the husbands and wives in common account for 8% of the variance. This suggests with respect to sex role that husband IQ contributes almost twice as much as wife IQ to the Interaction IQ. The contribution of husbands and wives jointly (8%) is not significantly different from zero.[1]

Is this effect of husbands and wives influenced by patient status? Table 3 indicates that it is. Husbands who are nonpatients are found to make the greatest contribution to Interaction IQ score ($r=.88$), while wives who are patients are least

TABLE 3: *Pearson Product-Moment Correlations between Individual IQ and Interaction IQ Scores of Husband Patient, Husband Nonpatient, Wife Patient, and Wife Nonpatient*

	Husbands	Wives
Nonpatients	.88 ($n = 28$)	.78 ($n = 22$)
Patients	.74 ($n = 22$)	.66 ($n = 28$)

influential ($r=.66$) ($t=2.06$, $p<.05$). This statistically significant difference indicates an interaction effect between husband-wife status and patient-nonpatient status in determining Interaction IQ.[2]

Analysis of Marital Interaction Process

A system of process analysis was developed using a comparison of individual and group products. The interaction process scoring system is based, for each Wechsler-Bellevue item, on a comparison of the Interaction Test response with the individual responses that had previously been produced by husband and wife alone. With this system, all interaction process can be subsumed under four categories: Dominance, Combination, Emergence, and Reinforcement.

Dominance is scored when the Interaction Test response contains one member's individual response in the absence of the other's individual response.

Combination is scored when elements of both members' responses, in whole or in part, are found in the Interaction Test response.

Emergence is scored for the presence of a new idea in the Interaction Test response.

Reinforcement occurs when the same response is given by both individuals and by husband and wife together.

The adequacy of interaction process is also scored by assigning the symbols $+$, $-$, and 0 to each process score. These are assigned operationally, simply by comparing the scores obtained on the three protocols for each item, that is, husband, wife, and Interaction.

Plus is scored when the Interaction score for the item compares favorably with the individual scores. It is, therefore, used when the Interaction score is equal to or higher than the better individual score. (In all three protocols, each response is scored as 2, 1, or 0, permitting these comparisons.)

0, or zero, is assigned to the item when the Interaction score is the same as both individual item scores.

The minus score is assigned when the Interaction response is poorer than the better individual response.

Clinical interests favored this type of scoring system, because it recorded not only such categories as dominance, reinforcement, etc., but it also characterized these processes as appropriate or inappropriate for the task at hand. We expected that such a characterization would have some reference to the concept of reality testing.

This system can be scored reliably, and agreement between independent raters is excellent.[3]

Table 4 presents reliability coefficients through comparison of Forms I and II, indicating the consistency with which couples are characterized by the different types of interaction process.

Each mean represents the number of instances of each process occurring in a total of 22 Wechsler-Bellevue items. (Consideration will not, in this paper, be given to the meaning of the distribution of means of the interaction process. These data require extensive analysis in view of the influence of the nature of the task and the scoring definitions.)

The consistencies of reliability coefficients, ranging from .48 to .84 are all significant beyond the .001 level. It thus appears that this scoring procedure, which in essence infers interaction process from a comparison of before and after products, pro-

TABLE 4: *Means, Standard Deviations, and Reliability Coefficients for Interaction Process Scores of 50 Married Couples on the Wechsler-Bellevue Intelligence Test, Forms I and II*

		DH	DW	D	C	E	R	−	+	0
M	I	7.92	5.28	13.20	1.20	5.34	3.06	4.86	6.56	10.58
	II	8.12	4.86	12.98	1.54	5.28	3.22	4.92	7.48	9.60
SD	I	3.71	3.07	2.81	1.26	2.71	1.63	2.23	2.01	2.16
	II	3.66	2.53	2.86	1.53	2.93	1.96	2.10	2.29	2.65
Reliability[a]		.76	.84	.54	.68	.71	.51	.48	.72	.57

Note. Abbreviations: DH = Husband dominance; DW = Wife dominance; D = Total dominance (DH + DW); C = Combination; E = Emergence; R = Reinforcement; − = Negative; + = Positive. For $N = 50$, $r_{.01} = .358$, $r_{.001} = .447$.
[a]Spearman-Brown correction.

duces significantly reliable ways of characterizing couples (although some of the reliabilities are too low for practical prediction).[4]

It is, thus, possible to characterize decision-making processes in couples in a way that may lend itself to the development of a taxonomy or diagnostic system for marital interaction. In addition, a reliable and practical method has been demonstrated for scoring a quality of couples that is called, and presumed to be, interaction process, and it has also been shown that this scoring procedure does consistently characterize these couples to a significant degree.

One can speculate that the Interaction decision-making process (here shown to be reliably characteristic of couples) may provide a direct-observation model for investigation of individual thinking and decision-making behavior. Do couples, for example, who more heavily utilize Combination in decision making reflect qualities of fear of commitment? Do they resolve fears of making errors through some compromise between conflicting views? On the other hand, do couples who manifest considerable ritualized Dominance behavior reflect an exaggerated need for structure of intolerance of ambiguity?

More immediately, this study points to a number of questions and, in some instances, to approaches for investigating them. In addition to the validity issues for the various IQ and process measures that have been outlined above, it would seem useful to study the effects of spousal role or social status (e.g., husband-wife; patient-nonpatient) and their interaction in various cultures and subcultures. To what extent are husband-wife differences socially determined, and how much (if any) is attributable to biological (sex) differences? Does patienthood continue to influence decision making when the individual is no longer formally a "patient"? Is problem-solving efficiency, that is, the degree to which the couple utilizes its inherent resources, related to marital harmony, effectiveness of child rearing, or a therapeutic prognosis for the couple? What is the relationship between power and competence in "normal" and "pathological" families? What of the Interaction Test behavior of family triads and larger groups?

Studies are now in progress testing "normal" couples, following up several "patient" couples and testing family triads which include husband, wife, and an adolescent child. It is anticipated that these will shed further light on the psychological organization of families and their members.

NOTES

1. The difference between unique contributions of members was even more dramatic when the more competent members' contributions were compared with the less competent ones. (Regression Equation: .626 MC + .072LC + .004LC)

   These results are consistent with those of Triandis (Triandis, Midsell, and Ewen, 1962) in that his dyadic contributions were consistently smaller than the unique contributions of members, warranting the comparable conclusion that while the individuals were important determinants of the dyadic result (originality), "the interaction between the two individuals improved the prediction . . . very little." (Triandis' formulas using more creative members versus less creative members were as follows:

   .448MCr + .334LCr — .115MCrLCr
   .264MCr + .502LCr — .112MCrLCr.)

   The present findings thus support those of Triandis in that the interaction effect (Individual A $\times$ Individual B) in all these regression equations is negligible, while the individual effects are significant. Thus, couples' joint effectiveness is essentially predictable from individual scores a priori, provided the population "weighting" for husbands and wives has already been determined.

2. The influence of sex, patient status, relative IQ, and recorder status upon dominance process scores is investigated in detail in Bauman and Roman (1966).

3. Two independent raters scored the results on a representative sample of 992 items, using the revised Administration and Scoring Manual (Bauman and Roman, 1964). There was full interrater agreement of 736 of the items (92.9%). Partial agreement on 35 items (4.4%) and disagreements on 21 of the items (2.7%) were easily resolved through discussion.

4. This approach represents a marked departure from the usual interaction process scoring approach as typified by Bales' Interaction Process Analysis, based on the actual verbal and nonverbal exchange between individuals. The Interaction Testing procedure infers process indirectly, through a comparison of individual with joint products. As such, it is more easily and quickly scored and does not require a process observer.

REFERENCES

Bauman, G., and Roman, M. Interaction testing: Administration and scoring manual, revised. Available from author, 1964.

Bauman, G., and Roman, M. Interaction testing in the study of marital dominance. *Family Process,* 1966, *2,* 230–242.

Faust, W. Group versus individual problem-solving. *Journal of Abnormal and Social Psychology,* 1959, *59,* 68–72.

Hoffman, J., and Arsenian, J. An examination of some models applied to group structure and process. *International Journal of Group Psychotherapy,* 1966, *14,* 131–153.

Jackson, D., and Satir, V. Family diagnosis and family therapy. In N. Ackerman (Ed.), *Exploring the base for family therapy,* New York Family Service Association of America, 1961. Pp. 29–51.

Lidz, T., Cornelison, A., Fleck, S., and Terry, D. The intrafamilial environment of the schizophrenic patient: VI. The transmission of irrationality. *American Medical Association Archives of Neurology and Psychiatry,* 1958, *79,* 305–316.

Lorge, I., and Solomon, H. Two models of group behavior in the solution of eureka-type problems. *Psychometrika,* 1955, *20,* 139–148.

Marquart, D. Group probem solving. *Journal of Social Psychology,* 1955, *41,* 103–113.

Restle, F., and Davis, J. The analysis of problems and prediction of group problem-solving. *Journal of Abnormal and Social Psychology,* 1963, *66,* 103–116.

Roman, M., and Bauman, G. Interaction testing: A technique for the psychological evaluation of small groups. In M. Harrower, P. Vorhaus, M. Roman, and G. Bauman (Eds., *Creative variations in the projective techniques.* Springfield, Ill.: Charles C Thomas, 1960. Pp. 93–138.

Taylor, D. Problem solving by groups. Proceedings of the XIV International Congress of Psychology. Amsterdam: North Holland Publishing, 1954.

Triandis, H., Midsell, E., and Ewen, R. Some cognitive factors affecting group creativity. *University of Illinois Group Effectiveness Research Laboratory: Technical Report,* No. 5, 1962.

Wechsler, D. *The measurement of adult intelligence.* (3rd ed.) Baltimore: Williams & Wilkins, 1944.

Wechsler, D. *The Wechsler-Bellevue intelligence scale,* Form II. New York: CAL Psychological Corporation, 1946.

Wynne, L., and Singer, M. Thought disorder and family relations of schizophrenics. *Archives of General Psychiatry,* 1963, *9,* 191–206.

Zwerling, I., and Wilder, J. An evaluation of the applicability of the Day Hospital to the treatment of acutely psychotic patients. *Israel Annals of Psychiatry and Related Disciplines,* 1964, *2,* 162–185.

Appendix: Psychological Tests

The page numbers above refer to discussions on the use of these tests in research on the family.

Name Index

220   *Name Index*

Subject Index

Adolescents and young adults
schizophrenic, 134, 136
sons, 145
Aggressive behavior in the family, 173–187; *see also* Families of psychiatric patients
Allocentric mode of perception, 105
Anthropology, 7
socialization studies, 125–127
Antipoverty legislation, 107
"Assortive mating"; *see* Homogamy
Athenian Institute of Anthropos, 164
Authority structure, 71, 128–129
in American society, 22
and authoritarian character, 24
and equalitarian family, 127
in lower class homes, 27
and power in family, 28

Balance theory of marriage, 14
Blind-date party, 25–26
Blue-collar families, 26–28, 107–115
aspirations of, 115
characteristics of, 108
child nurturing patterns, 109, 112, 113
cognitive style, 110
joys in marital life, 112
life style described, 113–115
perception of marriage roles, 111–112
views of married life, 113

Case history interview, 51, 53, 74
Causal process, 156–158, 160
Children
birth order, 120
in blue-collar families, 109, 112, 113, 115
as family scapegoat, 135–137
identical twins, 158
in primitive societies, 125
and siblings, 133, 136, 138
socialization, and family influence, 6, 128, 136, 137, 138, 140, 157–158
Cognitive dissonance theory, 14
Communication
behavioral, 7
in homogamous theory of marriage, 12
theory, 168
verbal, 7
see also Blue-collar families
Complementarity, 35, 45–61, 96–106
and dominance submissive needs, 79
in friendship, 12
in group dynamics, 19
in middle class family roles, 27, 51
and middle class in university, 51
in needs other than mate selection, 19
neurotic roles in, 11

221